TEACHER TRAINING
AND SPECIAL
EDUCATIONAL NEEDS

TEACHER TRAINING AND SPECIAL EDUCATIONAL NEEDS

EDITED BY JOHN SAYER AND NEVILLE JONES

CROOM HELM
London • Sydney • Dover, New Hampshire

©1985 John Sayer and Neville Jones
Croom Helm Ltd, Provident House, Burrell Row,
Beckenham, Kent BR3 1AT
Croom Helm Australia Pty Ltd, Suite 4, 6th Floor,
64-76 Kippax Street, Surry Hills, NSW 2010, Australia

British Library Cataloguing in Publication Data

Teacher training and special educational needs.
   1. Teachers, Training of   2. Exceptional
children − Education
I. Sayer, John   II. Jones, Neville
371.9'07   LB1732

   ISBN 0-7099-3379-7

Croom Helm, 51 Washington Street,
Dover, New Hampshire 03820, USA

Library of Congress Cataloging in Publication Data
Main entry under title:

Teacher training and special educational needs.

   Bibliography: p.
   1. Teachers − Training of − Europe − Congresses.
2. Teachers − In-service training − Europe − Congresses.
3. Teachers of handicapped children − Training of −
Europe − Congresses. I. Sayer, John, 1931-   .
II. Jones, Neville, 1930-   .
LB1723. T42   1985   370'.7'1   85-21340
ISBN 0-7099-3379-7

W 28281 /16.95 11.85

Printed and bound in Great Britain by Mackays of Chatham Ltd, Kent

CONTENTS

Part Three : Strategies for Training Provision

FOREWORD

This volume has been planned to appear at a decisive moment in British education, and to make a significant contribution to developments which await governmental backing. That was the original intention behind the writing seminar in June 1984 at Halifax House, Oxford, which was held to shape the present publication. We therefore wish to acknowledge our debt of gratitude in two directions. First, to those who participated at the Halifax House seminar, as discussants to each of the drafts now published as chapters in a coherent book, or who have been correspondents. They are mentioned in an appendix, and together with the actual writers represent a broad spectrum of positive thinking on this important topic. It was our concern to bring together the thinking of leading exponents of alternative strategies, from this country and others in the EEC; from ordinary and special schools and further education; from support services, local authorities and higher education. The chapters are written on behalf of all who were involved in a memorable exercise. Secondly, we record our gratitude to the European Communities, for a financial contribution to the Halifax House seminar and for the support and encouragement of the Bureau for Action in Favour of Disabled People, in the European Commission. Both the Seminar and its outcome in this book are a sequel to the European Forum on Integration, established in Otzenhausen, Germany, in May 1983 (Dahmen). There is nothing insular about the task of preparing ourselves as a teaching profession with others to respond to the needs of all children.

John Sayer
Neville Jones

INTRODUCTION   Training for Diversity: the Context for Change

John Sayer

Within two years, there have been promptings from ACSET, the
Advisory Committee on the Supply and Education of Teachers,
towards three major shifts of teacher-training policy, which
could together make sense at last of developing whole-school
and whole-community approaches to meeting special educational
needs.   First ACSET's checklist of requirements for initial
teacher-education has already been adopted, and that includes
preparing all teachers to contribute to the whole range of
pupils' needs (ACSET, August 1983).   Second, ACSET has
recommended that more specific training to respond to special
needs should be offered only to teachers already familiar with
the full range of pupils (ACSET, June 1984).   Third, a national
system for planning, funding and securing in-service education
and training (INSET) has been powerfully recommended, to make
it possible to translate the identified needs of schools and
localities into training budgets and provision (ACSET, August
1984). *

    The three belong together; and together they offer for the
first time a prospect of support, training and development for
what is now a national policy to educate all children as far as
possible in the ordinary school and in its full range of
activities.

    So the criteria recommended by ACSET for the use of the new
accreditation council (CATE) draw away from the common
practices of initial training for a single route in special

education, and towards co-operative modes of teaching in a complex community, with special educational needs as just one of the elements. Courses of initial education will now have to take account of the diversity and full range of pupils and their backgrounds, and of the flexibility of response required for each individual in a group. They will touch on child development and the different ways children learn; on assessment and expectation, learning difficulties and potential; on identification of special educational needs and the use of available resource and support; on group work and language exchange; on staff collaboration; on the inter-relationship of school and society, school and home, school and adult world; and on the classroom and its relationship with broader educational purposes.

Far from being a pipedream, all this is now in the pipeline. It is all accepted by government as a requirement; initial training courses will not be approved and accredited unless they can demonstrate that these elements are dealt with effectively. Teachers coming into the service by the 1990s will all have this as a common training background. However, this reform in isolation would leave untouched the great majority of teachers already in service, three-quarters of whom will be teaching our children's children in the next millenium. It also presents a challenge of maintaining and extending these elements of professional practice throughout a teaching career in rapidly changing circumstances. That is why ACSET's initiatives on in-service development are critically important, and why we must have approaches to training related to special educational needs seen very clearly as being in a context of the whole school and the whole range of local resources.

If this broad strategy is adopted, there is a prospect of all teachers and other professional workers seeing themselves as contributors to responses to special needs among others. The minorities who would previously have been segregated either by their specific professions or by the segregation of their client groups will adapt to being an additional resource not only to pupils with special needs but perhaps even more to their teachers, working alongside them to extend access to normal school programmes, and to extend what has been thought normal so that it becomes more accessible to all pupils. Not much of that is likely to happen until those with specialised resource skills have also had a trained background of experience in the mainstream; and this of course is the starting point of the new ACSET recommendations.

There are plenty of difficulties in this approach. For one thing, it is much more difficult to identify staffing needs. In a segregated model, guidelines were easy to draw up and easy to check. The DES Circular 4/73 recommended one specialist

2

teacher per group of six younger children with hearing impairment, or eight such older children; there were much the same ratios for the blind and partially sighted, the autistic, those with speech and language impairment. For moderate learning difficulties, the ratio was to be one to eleven, for severe cases, one to nine; for the physically handicapped and epileptic, one to eight or ten, down to one to four and five for the most severe cases; and for the maladjusted, one to seven through to one per three or four psychotic cases. The two main ingredients were specialist skills and staff contact time. In special schools and units other than those for children with hearing or visual impairment only a small minority of teachers still have had specialist training at all; most are specialists only in the sense that they give most of their time to teaching children with these special needs.

Circular 4/73 is out of date, and ACSET has called for urgent attention to criteria for staffing in the new variety of settings. We know very little indeed about the staffing levels required to meet all needs in an ordinary school setting (Sayer, 1982). Until we know better, we have to assume that equivalent levels should apply whatever may be the local model of provision. However, one marked difference is that this additional resource for specialised work will have to be trained, and indeed trained for a whole-school and community education model, as one of the likely future contexts, in fact the one to which we are now committed in policy and law. Far from diminishing the emphasis on specialist training at present required for work only with hearing and visual needs, ACSET's recent recommendations add significantly to the training requirement, across the whole range of needs. A teacher with no more than general training and commitment may cope in a specialised unit; but to be a resource in an open team, greater emphasis on specialised skills will be looked for by colleagues.

This poses another question, which is taken up in several chapters of this book. Do we want in any one school or group of schools a distinct body of specific professionals whose sole activity is to be a specialist resource to others or to children with special needs, and who therefore lose much of their initial training as 'ordinary' teachers? It is a dilemma facing others already: professional tutors, school counsellors, deputy heads, or advisers. In order to keep abreast of general practice and be seen to do so, teachers who have developed specialist skills as a resource to others may well need to maintain their work as 'ordinary' teachers too. If they do so for only a third of their programme, that means offering specialist training to half as many teachers again, and it also demands more of school organisations and management.

3

It is most urgent, therefore, that training needs of different kinds should be identified and quantified: for specialist teachers to help meet specific needs; for teachers trained as a resource for general learning difficulties; for subject specialists, particularly in secondary schools, to help their departments adapt and extend learning materials and teaching styles; for resource group leaders within and across schools and colleges; and for heads, advisers and officers as part of management training.

That is why the proposals relating to training and special educational needs depend on ACSET's model for INSET as a whole. There has to be a coherent scheme for England and Wales which ensures that identified needs are met by training opportunities. At present there is a general acceptance of the notions associated with school-focused in-service education, in which working groups and individuals seek to identify training needs and priorities to improve their effectiveness in each situation, and seek support from local authorities and training institutions beyond the school to help develop a range of INSET activities. The booklet *Making Inset Work* (DES, 1978), distributed some years ago from the DES to all schools, sets out a catechism for the purpose; but this bears no relationship yet to the funding mechanisms for INSET, either from central or local government. The move to INSET for all specific forms of training to meet special educational needs therefore requires a radical reform of the whole INSET machinery, of the kind now proposed.

Certainly in this respect, the Audit Commission's recent comments on local government financing are right. Something like a three year cycle of management is required for schools to identify needs and draw up proposals to be agreed and provision planned in the most appropiate contexts; for funding to be allocated and courses laid on; and for evaluation which in turn will modify the next cycle of decisions. INSET should not depend on annual hiccups of 104 different authority budgets. A national policy to allocate something like five per cent of teachers' salary budgets to this purpose, and to set up area professional committees as brokers across LEAs and training institutions, would seem to be essential if opportunities wherever they happen to be employed are to become comparable, and the needs of children wherever they happen to be in school are to be met.

So the shift towards INSET for training related to specialised responses to special educational needs is in line with shifts in the training and development patterns for the teaching profession as a whole. Funds previously mandated for a higher proportion of intial training must be transferred, and new money added to put policy into practice. Instead of mandatory qualifications only for sight and hearing, there should be a required level of provision for trained specialists right through the service. Finally, from the area professional committees we should be looking for a model of professional co-operation to reflect the wholeness of the education service to the public.

The Topic and Title

The title of this volume implies nothing more than acceptance that 'training' and 'special educational needs' are part of contemporary language. There are overtones, which are rightly identified in subsequent chapters, but they are not the overtones of this publication. Briefly, *training* may be narrowly conceived in behaviourist terms, with a sense of the teacher as a passive recipient being modified by systematic treatment, or being dragged along by the power of some other force than the teacher's own. In other contexts, it may be used in a restricted sense to contrast with general education, as a course undergone to acquire vocational skills and drills. On the other hand, training is a generic term to cover the whole field of selection, induction, development including self-development, appraisal including self-appraisal, and career promotion. It can therefore be even wider than teacher education. Current usage is loose and inconsistent; and courses of training are a part of the wider sense of professional development anyway. Most writers in this volume, we believe, would tend towards the wider rather than the narrower connotations.

So too, our acceptance of 'special educational needs' is no more than acceptance of current means of communication. None of us is likely to describe children as 'special needs children'; we are all determined to respond to and reduce needs to a minimum; some of us would wish to move away from both the term and the focus as a next stage towards seeing all needs met by appropriate resource and response; and the very notion of 'needs' as a basis for educational planning and response may be questioned even while we use the language of the day. Even among contributors, there are a wide range of perceptions underlying the use of our title.

A Forum of Positive Thinking

It was precisely the wish to bring together the widest possible range of positive responses to ACSET's proposals for teacher-training related to special educational needs which prompted the Halifax House seminar and this volume. We were all too aware of the pressure of special pleading, much of it resistant to the change and impervious to the public will to bring together the separate sections and interest-groups of an

education service, which had been suffered by the working party
set up by ACSET in September 1983. We wanted to explore the
differences of opinion and interpretation among those who want
new concepts and policies to be translated into practice, and
to expose the real issues and challenges to be faced in
responding to the ACSET proposals. To do so, we have felt it
necessary to draw on all parts of the education service and on
related professions, and to take soundings from those who are
not caught in the immediate context of England and Wales. What
this volume offers, therefore, is a response not from any one
consultative body or interest, but we believe from a
significant sample of thinking practitioners right across the
service and across frontiers. We are trying to move the debate
on from Warnock and the 1981 Act, on from the ACSET
discussions, to the stage of implementing proposals, of
marrying concept and practice.

This is presented in three parts. In the first, some of
the major issues of changing contexts are highlighted and
confronted. Tony Booth invites us to consider directions,
philosophy and progress towards a comprehensive education
service and away from current contradictions. Neville Jones
explores the fundamental shift of attitudes to handicap or
disability which has to be shared if the rhetoric of conceptual
change is to be enacted. Dennis Mongon takes us through the
variety of patterns of service delivery for which training must
prepare, whilst I concentrate on the transformation of the
'mainstream' rather than the 'ordinary' school of yesterday.

The second part of the book opens with a penetrating
challenge by Patricia Potts, exposing what may be meant by
teamwork before considering the role of training for it. David
Thomas and Colin Smith remind us that the general contribution
of initial training cannot be left to generalities, and show
training institutions, like schools, exploring the combined
offerings of subject specialists and tutors who have
specialised in special education. Klaus Wedell moves us
through the range of service requirements to be developed
through post-experience training, and sets out the nature of
INSET provision required for each aspect, distinguishing
clearly between roles and relating training to organisation and
management. Nanette Whitbread reminds us of the extension of
mainstream provision required for the post-sixteen age-group,
and of the training needs of a partly untrained further
education staff. The section concludes with a view from across
the Channel, a reminder from Dominique Paty that we may be
trapped in the language of special education, and a look at
interpretations abroad.

Finally, we consider strategies for training and the
priorities for training agencies and services. John Quicke

sets out the new contributions to be made by support services, in a chapter which may be read as a response to Patricia Potts. Michael Jones develops further the whole-school approach, dwelling on the training role of the school and coming down firmly on the side of curriculum development as the key to an integrated approach. Marion Blythmans's case-study from Scotland both records the impressive reform which has already been carried out there, and sets out the questions raised for later developments south of the border. Tim Southgate has an important chapter on the training contribution of micro-technology, which together with Tony Booth's exposition of training through distance learning serves to complete the range of available training resources required to bring about a major reform in our own generation. Neville Jones concludes with what we have learnt from each other in the Halifax House seminar, and with pointers for the future.

This volume is written for all who are involved in teacher-education, whether in training institutions, schools or local authorities, and for those working in special education whose skills can become a resource to the whole service. It contains chapters and case-studies which will be valuable for training courses, particularly of more advanced study. It offers answers to the simple question: once the ACSET recommendations on teacher-training and special educational needs become accepted policy, what do we do?

Chapter One

IN-SERVICE TRAINING AND PROGRESS IN SPECIAL EDUCATION

Tony Booth

In this chapter I will argue that before in-service training
can make a contribution to progress in special education we
have to be clear about what constitutes progress.   Since
progress can only be defined in terms of moral and political
goals any particular initiatives have to be examined for
their underlying philosophy and practical consequences so
that a choice can be made between them.   What kinds of
schools do they support or tend to produce? I will look at
the way the moral and political choices in education are
obscured by the needs of educators to claim neutrality.   I
will then examine the 'new' approach to special education
which has followed the Warnock report and 1981 Education Act
and is characterised by such slogans as 'Every teacher a
teacher of special needs', ' A whole school approach', 'An
expanded notion of special needs'.   I will suggest   that it
contains contradictory elements, with their own history which
require analysis before they should be adopted. The approach
may owe more to a selective philosophy than one compatible
with the long-term development of the comprehensive school.
Finally I will indicate a conception of special education
which is compatible with the enhancement of a 'comprehensive'
non-selective education in primary and secondary schools.

Progress and Politics in Education

Even if we make the assumption that progressive change within
schools can be facilitated through in-service training, the
simple provision of *more* training cannot of itself lead to
progress.   For progress is change in accordance with our
moral and political values.   In a society in which people
differ markedly about the way of life, including the style
and content of schooling they desire, there can be no
consensus about the nature of progress nor about the means to
foster it.   Special educators cannot be pictured as a single
community of benevolent gardeners tending a common plot of

special education, each contributing to compatible corners of scented beauty. One should consider the possibility instead, that some might like to cultivate sunflowers while others specialise in bind weed though the identities of each of these group would depend on one's perspective. In gardening, weeds are plants which you don't want to see on your patch.

The notion that change can and should be achieved through consensus remains attractive. It implies that disagreement within education can be resolved despite major political differences and may appear to offer a way out of an interminable need to push one's own case against opposing forces. However I would suggest that such a notion only obscures the nature of educational change and can be counterproductive. While some of us wait for consensus to be reached others will be fashioning education for their own ends. Further, the emergence of an apparent consensus within a professional group, which suppresses differences in basic philosophy, may work against the interests of the population it is meant to serve. For consensus may be achieved on the basis of a shared professional interest. It can be argued that the advancement of professional power is at the expense of the power of the client group.

If we wish to make progress in education, we need to have a vision of the way we would like education to be developed as well as an understanding of the implications for changes in current practice that this entails. The value on any intervention in education can be assessed, in part, by the extent to which it contributes to desired moral and political ends. Now I am putting this forward as purely an option for the 'ideologues'. I am suggesting that it is a necessary condition for intelligent action in education. In her philosophical role Mary Warnock has argued:

> ...understanding things imaginatively is itself a deep source of pleasure and satisfaction. But it is also the only possible way to intelligent action. In order to see how things can or should be changed, it is necessary first to know what they are, even how they came to be as they are...
>
> Imagination, then, is what enables one both to understand how things are, and to raise the question Need they remain like this? and How could they be different?
>
> (Warnock, 1978, pp.8-9)

But this imaginative mental overview of practice and

possibility cannot make our actions intelligent by itself. We have to make the 'right' choices and to do that we have to assess possibilities against the standard of principles.

But surely even if a view of education as politics can be sustained for mainstream education, it is strangely out of place within special education? In special education there is a widespread belief that the provision of appropriate education can depend on the neutral identification of educational needs discovered by assessment of individual pupils. A debate about the functions of special schools within a selective and stratifying system of education can be avoided for example, by arguing pupils should be placed in accordance with their individual needs; that it is quality rather that place of education which is the important issue (Brennan, 1982). By focusing on the needs of the child it is thought that we may discover that he or she needs a particular placement. Such an argument relies on a mistaken analogy with basic bodily requirements and presumes that the connection between educational need and its satisfaction is as unproblematic as the connection between hunger and food. Yet it should be clear that the content and organisation of schooling for all pupils raise similar questions. What should they learn? How should they learn?

The idea that debates such as those about selection and comprehensive education and about racist and sexist curricula do not apply within special education is itself a form of segregation which has overtones of ineducability. Yet a consideration of the educational consequences of the sex, class or colour of pupils is of particular relevance to special education. All categories of special school have a majority of boys and the preponderance in maladjusted schools is overwhelming (DES Statistics, 1982). The disproportionate number of black pupils in disruptive units or recommended for ESM(M) provision remains a cause of argument and conflict (Tomlinson, S. 1981). Virtually all pupils sent to schools for pupils with moderate learning difficulties or day maladjusted provisions are working class (Tomlinson, 1982). Recently a further issue has resurfaced to my consciousness with relative numbers of men and women taking courses about 'special needs'. In the first three years of the Open University course 'Special Needs in Education', 78 per cent of students were women. Some people might go further than proposing that these issues should be on the agenda of special education by suggesting that they are the agenda; that the significance of special education lies in the way pupils (and possibly teachers) are categorised, stratified and differentially valued.

The fact that advocacy of a particular change in

education is also the advancement of moral and political ends can appear to be terribly inconvenient in our education system. Education is meant to be steered by politically neutral experts, DES officials, HMI and teachers. Of course such an assumption involves an interesting view of processes within the structure of the Department of Education and Science. At exactly what point in such a structure is political influence filtered out of the system? After all, the political party in power would see its role of education as the introduction of political bias into the system and this might be most clearly detected by overt efforts to remove contrary views. The involvement of the DES hierarchy at the level of HMI in the political control of what should be taught in schools is suggested for example in a statement by Pauline Perry, Chief HMI, about an in-service training course in peace studies: 'we never intervene in actual topics - although I think we might have done in this case' (Guardian, 28th July 1984). The independence that HMI do have has been challenged by recent attempts to question their right to examine the effects of government spending cuts in education (TES, October 5th 1984). The moves to greater central political control of the curriculum has been widely discussed elsewhere (see for example Lawton, 1980, 1984). Actions do not have to carry a party label to be political. All actions which sustain a particular way of life are political and they do not cease to be simply because the life they support has majority approval or is really questioned.

But because political neutrality is often assumed in the job description of educators they have become adept at concealing their reasons for advocating or disparaging certain changes. At times this sets them off on false though self-perpetuating trails to find non-political answers to political questions. For example, the question 'what is a good school?', although beloved by researchers, actually lies outside the province of research. Thousands of working days have been devoted to the attempt to find the school ethos which produces successful law-abiding citizens with different researchers arguing for 'tight ships' or 'happy families' (Rutter, et.al, 1979; Reynolds, et.al, 1981). Yet our preferred ethos for schools is not 'caused' by a relationship with so-called outcome measures. On the contrary the outcomes we expect as well as the means we employ to achieve them depend on the way we wish to run our schools.

Research is introduced, then, as the neutral middle-person in supporting change. We await the results of research before we say that 'research has shown that....' so it must be desirable. We also like to lean on laws; 'We should do it because it's in the 1981 Act'. Yet we know that educational law rarely contains precise prescriptions and that there are good laws and bad laws. Our belief in the general value that laws should be obeyed may lead to a game over interpretation of laws between advocates of opposing view. Since the enactment of the 1981 Act the argument over whether or not the Act implies greater integration of pupils from special schools has appeared at times like a touring Punch and Judy show. 'The 1981 Act is an integrationist Act' - 'oh no it isn't...,etc. The real issue, of course, is whether or not integration should be supported rather than whether or not the Act can supply an escape from that moral dilemma.

But perhaps the most prevalent way for avoiding or concealing moral responsibility involves an appeal to historical inevitability; that's the way things are going; schools are going to have to be more accountable; the technological revolution is coming. Such a view has two poles: positive and negative; inevitable progress or unavoidable disaster. Pritchard's history of special education emphasises the former view. He outlines the succession of stages in the education of handicapped children - from earliest provision through the periods of experiment, transition, state intervention, growth and consolidation. Reading his account it seems as if progress has been guaranteed by the benevolence of history:

> Progress there has been; progress from that day in 1760 when Thomas Braidwood first used his spatula-like instrument to a day two hundred years later, when the Department of Education of the Deaf at Manchester advertised for a research fellow with qualifications in physics or electrical engineering. Progress there must yet be; progress in overcoming the problems that still exist in every aspect of the field of special education.

> (Pritchard, 1963, p. 221)

The vision of society as a diabolical machine careering towards disaster beyond human control is conveyed in Zola's 'La Bete Humaine' with the metaphor of the driverless train carrying soldiers into battle:

> Now out of control, the engine tore on and on...What did the victims matter that the machine destroyed on its way? Wasn't it bound for the future. heedless of spilt blood? With no human hand to guide it through the night, it roared on and on, a blind and deaf beast let loose amid

> death and destruction, laden with cannon-fodder...
>
> (Zola, 1890, pp. 365-6)

Both images of education, as a hurtling and unstoppable train heading for disaster or as constituted in the march of progress depict teachers as a compliant force, maintenance engineers or 'cannon fodder', with little interest in or contribution to make to the direction in which they travel. Yet it is the assumption of this book that teachers and other educators influence schooling. It is the main argument of this chapter that if we are to know what we are doing we have to link our day to day actions with an overall philosophy of education.

What is New in Special Education?

In examining the contribution of in-service training to progress we need to look carefully, then, at the content of courses, at the view of education which underlies them and the practices within schools which they encourage and sustain. The approach we adopt should be one that is compatible with our desired ends. Now, current literature on special education assumes that there is a new approach to special education associated with the 1978 Warnock Report (DES, 1978) and the 1981 Education Act (DES, 1981) which has been described in some sections of official circles as radical or even revolutionary. Without any precise specifications of this 'new' approach we are all meant to regard it as progressive and implement it in our practice. In fact some books and in-service initiatives have responded to the inevitable mental confusion which arises from taking such an attitude to official documents by passing on the messages of Report and Act as if they were coherent and clear (see Brennan, 1982a). The effect that such a tactic is likely to have on the mental states of any but the most independent minded of the recipients of such messages is likely to be anything but educational.

An End to Categorisation

We are now meant to see difficulties and disabilities in education as part of a seamless continuum, as argued in a recent in-service training package:

> As categorisation of handicapped pupils promotes confusion between a child's disability and the form of special education he needs, the report firmly recommends its abolition. This removes any statutory distinction between handicapped and non-handicapped and allows the focus to be centred on

the child himself rather than on his disability. It emphasises the fact that children with learning difficulties display limitless patterns of individual strengths and weaknesses along a wide continuum of need.

(Leeson and Foster, 1984, p. 10)

Yet we are also meant to have the precise numbers of 'special' and 'special-needs' children fixed firmly in our heads:

The report actually makes the conclusion that about one in six children at any time, and up to one in five children at some time during their career will require some form of special educational provision.

This means that out of every 100 children in the ordinary school, 20 will have special educational needs and of these only 1 or 2 require special schooling.

(Leeson and Foster, 1984, p. 9)

The Warnock Report contained a section headed 'A new system to replace categorisation' but also argued for the collection of statistics about children with disabilities according to traditional categories distinguished by five levels of severity. In fact the new form 7 introduced by the DES transformed the five levels of severity into three levels of ability (DES, 1984a). In California, there was a similar attempt to replace old categories by the phrase 'individuals with exceptional needs'. Teachers began referring to 'IWEN's', making them sound like little beings from outer space (Booth, 1982).

Along with the new injunction to end categorisation we must identify which pupils have special needs as early as possible. Although there were attempts within the recent ACSET sub-committee to discuss the needs of education rather than the needs of children, there are passages in the ACSET report which encourage the early identification of children with special needs as a separate group.

All teachers of the 2-19 age group need to know how to identify the special educational needs of children and young people, what they can do to meet these needs and when and how to enlist

15

> specialist help...Many teachers in ordinary schools who have pupils with special educational needs in their classes are ill-equipped to ensure that these needs are met.
>
> (ACSET), 1984, pp. 2-3)

New Definitions

We must learn and inwardly digest (and chant in unison?) the 1981 Act definitions until their familiarity causes us to forget problems about their sense, let alone their sexist language:

> For the purposes of this Act a child has "special educational needs" if he has a learning difficulty which calls for special educational provision to be made for him.
>
> A child has a "learning difficulty" if he has a significantly greater difficulty in learning than the majority of children of his age; or he has a disability which either prevents or hinders him from making use of educational facilities of a kind generally provided in schools.
>
> When learning difficulties reach the point at which additional or alternative provision is required they give rise to special educational needs.
>
> (Leeson and Foster, 1984, p. 11)

Within a single sentence learning difficulties are defined as a deviation from a population norm and, for pupils with disabilities, as relative to the provision in an LEA. In both cases learning difficulties are the property of pupils which stretches ordinary language considerably when applied to a gifted child in a wheelchair who has not been provided with ramps to enter a school building.

All Teachers of Special Needs

We embrace the slogan 'every teacher a teacher of special needs' and turn it into an objective of in-service training (Muncey and Ainscow, 1982). We adopt a whole school approach to learning difficulties echoing the Bullock report's view of language teaching across the curriculum (DES, 1975), but we may not specify the approaches we are all to take unless, of course, it is behavioural objectives. These were imported from mainstream education in the USA into special education in the UK and are now to be spread from there across the curriculum. They are often taken to be part of the essence of the official new approach to special education embracing in one fell swoop a modern approach to both ordinary and special education:

> The technique of modern curriculum development and design have not been widely applied to the curriculum for slow learners...the technique is outlined as the reduction of general curriculum aims to the statements of behavioural objectives at intermediate and terminal points in the curricular process...
>
> (Brennan, W., 1974, p. 96)

Without going into a detailed account of the advantages and disadvantages of behaviourist theory, practice and terminology in education (Swann, 1983) it should be clear that the spread of behaviourist approaches depends on a particular view of teachers, pupils and their relationship in education which many reject (see, for example, Holt, 1981). Their use has something to say, too, in the UK context at least, of about where models of good practice are to be derived for all teachers now that 'every teacher is a teacher of special needs'. Should 'the approach' be about the expansion of the methods and techniques of special education or the extension of ideas of collaborative teaching and learning within diverse groups in the common school?

What is the Expanded Notion of Special Education?

What is said to be 'new' in the approach to special education may consist of contradictory elements and may have its own long history. In this respect the idea of an 'expanded notion of special education' is particularly interesting both because of its age and also because current confusions and contradictions in its use can be detected in earlier formulations. The Wood committee on mental deficiency (1929) recognised the existence in ordinary schools of a wider group of children who had problems similar to those of children in special schools and expanded its remit:

> The scheme we propose involves to some extent a fresh orientation in our conceptions and a fresh terminology. We are no longer concerned only with children who have been actually certified...indeed we contemplate the abolition of such certification ... we have in mind all

> those other children of similar grade and
> educational capacity who ... are properly
> certified
> and further the still larger group of dull or
> backward children.

(Wood Report, 1929, p. 126)

To what extent have current conceptions of special needs
moved away from ideas about the dull or backward? Cyril Burt
who sat on the Wood Committee persistently drew attention to
the falsity of a sharp distinction between the normal and
abnormal:

> Between the normal and the subnormal there is no
> sharp line of cleavage...In the past the practice
> of medicine has been apt to regard the healthy and
> the sick as forming separate groups, and to
> recognise no link between the two...Nowhere is
> this love of sorting people into sharply
> contrasted types more prevalent and more
> misleading than in psychology. We shall meet it
> again and again. If at the very outset we insist
> that all men must be either normal or abnormal, we
> are bound to ask - Is any one perfectly normal?

(Cyril Burt, 1935, p. 3)

Echoing the Wood Report, he drew attention to the large
number of borderline pupils:

> Every medical officer who has the duty of
> examining defectives soon becomes aware of
> borderline dullards whom he cannot conscientiously
> certify; and he quickly discovers that these
> marginal cases consist, not of a few problematic
> individuals, cropping up from time to time, but of
> an unexpectedly large proportion of the
> population.

(Cyril Burt, 1935, p 113)

In reading these quotations one might be tempted to
think that Burt was actually suggesting that strict
categorisation of pupils by ability was impossible. Yet apart
from what we know about the advocacy of selection and
streaming in the 'Black' papers he does juxtapose a precise
division between the inherently defective and the merely dull
and educationally retarded alongside his more liberal view:

> Formerly, the education officer congratulated the

> special school teacher on the number of cases
> retransferred as normal; now he is more likely to
> blame the doctor for a mistaken diagnosis. The
> majority of these transfers prove to be children
> whose inborn intellegence is just above the line
> of certification...
>
> (Burt, 1935, pp. 114-115)

This double standard, that there both is and is not a
clear distinction between the handicapped and non-handicapped
persists, as I have suggested echoed in the language of
special needs. The role of such a distinction in sustaining a
selective philosophy for mainstream schools is obscured by
our apparent commitment to its abolition.

A Curriculum Led Model for Special Needs

In the last three years a number of people and HMI in
particular, have advocated that the categorisation of pupils
by disability could be replaced by a categorisation by
curricular needs and this has emerged as part of the system
of gathering statistics about pupils in special schools
through the use of form 7M (Fish, 1984) (DES, 1984a). Pupils
in special schools are said to need one of three kinds of
curriculum; mainstream plus support, modified and
developmental. However it is clear that what is termed
curricular needs actually involves categorisation by ability.
Mainstream plus support means a curriculum like that provided
in ordinary schools but with the provision of additional
resources; modified means appropriate to children with
moderate learning difficulties; developmental means designed
for children with severe learning difficulties (DES, 1983,
pp. 1-2). These ideas arose from a need to establish a new
basis on which to categorise special schools. After all,
their rationale had depended on the idea that appropriate
education required the division of pupils and schooling
according to disability. A movement away from categorisation
of school by disability left a need for a new form of
justification if they were to be retained. Within the British
educational system categorisation and schooling by ability
still appears natural particularly in relation to those
pupils of lower ability omitted from moves towards
comprehensive education.

Circular 10/65 (DES, 1965) which described the push
towards schooling across the whole ability range actually
coincided with the maximum growth in provision for pupils of
low ability. Without the presumed underpinning of an implicit
natural selection or school centred education, the idea of
three kinds of curricular need would have little credence. It

19

has been suggested that no special school should be expected to cope for more than one of these curricular needs or levels (for example, Green 1982). Yet within a comprehensive primary or secondary school how many curricular needs could one identify? It is the purpose of such schools to cater for diverse needs and interests within a shared curriculum. It is interesting that it is not suggested that all or necessarily the majority of pupils who are to receive a curriculum entitled mainstream plus support should actually receive their education within mainstream schools. According to one draft HMI document outlining future provision for pupils with physical disabilities it was suggested that secondary pupils should receive their 'mainstream plus support' curriculum in boarding schools!

Partnership with Parents

The contradictory notions of our new approach are well represented by the exhortations to professionals to offer a new partnership to parents. We are told that collaboration is...one of the hallmarks of a well-trained professional and that children will develop and learn better if parents and professionals are working together on a basis of equality than if either is working in isolation (Mittler and Mittler, 1982, p. 7). But what would equality with parents entail? Would it involve them in having a say in what decisions are to be taken about their children and the people who should participate in such decision making as well as the way decisions should be reached? In many partnerships there are junior and senior partners. At present there is more encouragement to parents to participate in a plan defined by teachers and other professionals than to define a policy themselves. This is highlighted by the parental contribution to statementing procedures. Seen by some as an increase in parental rights in education the statementing process restricts the rights of parents over choice of school for their children compared to others and tends to limit their contribution to what may seem an incomprehensible set of procedures.

The DES is contemplating further circumscribing the contribution of parents by developing a standard form for parents on which they can submit their assessment of their child's needs (DES, 1984b). I find it interesting that in their booklet the Mittlers do not discuss any parent initiated groups such as Family Focus (1982), nor do they mention the issue of integration. Even though their account is restricted, primarily, to a discussion of parents and professionals in relation to mental handicap the issue of integration has been placed very firmly on the agenda of such parents by themselves and particularly within the Down's

Children's Association (Burrows, 1983).

Moving Towards Integration?

We must all now support integration whilst retaining special schools and finding new roles for them:

> Mainstream schools should not be considered as alternatives to special schools, for both kinds of provision are necessary in any comprehensive system of special education.

> (Brennan, 1982b, p. 29)

Is it a comprehensive system of education or a comprehensive system of special education for which we are aiming? Certainly some people appear to advocate integration whilst focusing on its drawbacks:

> Many children with special educational needs should be educated in ordinary schools...

> Examination of resource commitment between special and ordinary school provision provides a contrast of effort and neglect...It is undeniable that the concentration of expensive specialised resources in one place and the feeding in to that place of children who need the resources, has been exceptionally effective in meeting the personal needs of handicapped pupils, especially when contrasted with the almost complete absence of the necessary resources in ordinary schools.

> (Brennan, 1982b, p. 42, p. 10)

Of course the quality of provision within special schools can vary dramatically from school to school (see for example HMI report on College Park School, DES, 1984). But it is simply misleading to attempt to prime the readers reaction by contrasting good provision under one system with poor provision under another. The decision about which ordinary, human, messy system one wishes to advocate depends on one's overall attitudes towards it (Booth, Potts and Swann, 1983).

Many of us believe integration is occurring yet according to the most recent national figures the proportion of pupils in segregated special schools is still rising as it has for the last thirty years (Booth, 1981; Swann, 1985). We may even be encouraged to think of the natural population of special schools as 2 percent, a figure which has not yet been reached in the UK:

> Although it is recognised that most children will
> then be educated in ordinary schools, there will
> be a small percentage of children, about 2% who
> will have severe or complex learning difficulties
> and who will require special schooling.

(Leeson and Foster, 1984, p. 12)

It is interesting that just as some people have ascribed
an integration intent to the Warnock Report and 1981
Education Act which is unfounded (Booth, 1981) others have
claimed a similar intent in the Wood Report of 1929:

> Far greater integration of mentally handicapped
> children in ordinary elementary schools was one of
> the central recommendations of the Wood
> Committee...

(Sutherland, 1984, p.278)

In fact, the Wood Committee ordered a survey of the
incidence of mental deficiency in the population and found
that it had increased. They argued for an expansion of
provision to cater for the large numbers of hitherto
undetected children as well as the new group of retarded
children to be included within special education. They
wanted low grade children to be moved out of special schools
into occupation centres but felt that:

> The numbers of institutions and centres is totally
> inadequate and must be increased, especially when
> regard is had to the far larger numbers of
> children who, in our view, should be notified in
> the future.

(Wood Report, 1929, pp.69-70)

They argued that the presence of such children often
impedes the work of the special schools. If these were
removed then according to the report one of the chief factors
that had hampered the growth and efficiency of day special
schools would be eliminated. But it was the abolition of the
clear distinction, marked by certification, between the
deficient and the retarded that would enable the greatest
expansion:

> The other proposal, namely that the children
> admitted to these schools need not in the future
> be certified as mentally defective, is of still
> greater importance...it will result in the

> advantage of Day Special School Education being
> extended to retarded children...Not only will the
> schools now described as Day Special Schools
> receive many more pupils but Education Authorities
> who hitherto have felt that there were not
> sufficient children whom they could certify as
> mentally defective to form such a school, will no
> doubt adopt a different view and make provision
> for retarded children.

(Wood Report, 1929, p.133)

The members of the committee felt that this expansion in
provision might be restricted to the towns at primary level
where numbers made it viable but at secondary level they
hoped that special school provision could be extended in many
areas where it had not been possible previously. They
clearly linked the separation and expansion of a special
school sector to selection at age eleven:

> This provision will be made not only for the
> majority of children of the grade now attending
> these senior day special schools, but also for the
> large numbers of other retarded children who show
> no aptitude for the ordinary school subjects; and
> these latter children can be included in the
> future because under our scheme there will be no
> necessity for certification. The schools we
> contemplate will form one group of the post-
> primary or central schools.

(Wood Report, 1929, p.135)

Special Education and Selection

In my discussion of the new approach to special education I
have emphasised the ideas about selection in education which
lie behind it. According to a selective philosophy it is
thought to be desirable and possible to divide pupils into
homogeneous groups for teaching purposes based on the
characteristics of the pupils. On such a view difficulties
in learning are seen to arise, primarily, because of defects
or deficiencies in pupils rather than in the curriculum and
organisation of ordinary schools:

> A child's special needs may result from
> difficulties in physical, sensory, social,
> intellectual and emotional development or, indeed,
> from some combination of these.

(Coventry LEA, 1982, p.4)

23

Just as it was naive or insincere to suggest that education for black pupils in the southern states of the USA could be 'separate but equal' it would be disingenuous not to see how the creation of 'pupils with special needs' can be part of a selective and stratifying philosophy in which different bands of pupils are assigned a different value. After the assertion of the benefits of comprehensive education by parents in Solihull government effort has become directed at selection within schools. As Sir Keith Joseph remarked in a television interview, 'If it be so, as it is, that selection as between schools is largely out - then I emphasise that there must be differentiation within schools'.

It seems that the ideas, concepts and terminology used within special education are so deeply rooted in practices of selection that it has become impossible to formulate an alternative approach within them. According to the 1981 Education Act special provision is that which is not made generally available in schools. Ordinary schools are considered to provide an education geared to the 'normal' learner and those pupils who do not or cannot conform to the definition of normality embodied in such schooling are said to have learning difficulties.

But perhaps the most revealing feature of the new approach is shown by the exclusion from the definition of learning difficulty in the 1981 Act of those children whose language or form of the language spoken at home is different from that taught in school. Presumably the exclusion of such children from the Act despite the all-embracing definition of learning difficulty and special provision within the Act, occurs because there is a wish to avoid, for them, the stigmatising label of special needs. Is this an indication that the writers of the Act did interpret special needs to mean dull and backward? For if one would wish to avoid a stigmatising label for some children, shouldn't one avoid it for *all* children?

If, instead, schooling is viewed as a response to diversity, learning difficulties are seen to result from a mismatch between pupils and curricula. On this view, the number of pupils with special needs is not seen as a fixed quantity of the school population but reflects the success with which schools adapt curricula to a diversity of abilities, backgrounds, interests and needs. On such a view the achievement of progress in special education becomes part of a general effort to enhance the comprehensive nature of provision in nursery, primary and secondary education.

Chapter Two

ATTITUDES TO DISABILITY: A TRAINING OBJECTIVE

Neville Jones

This chapter is concerned with human attitudes, prejudicial or otherwise, which shape the responses that individuals make to those who in some respect do not fit within the cultural boundaries set by a given social group. The recipients are those children who in our society we refer to as the disabled, mentally, physically and behaviourally, whose disability may or may not be educationally handicapping.

Broadly, the term attitude, according to the Oxford Dictionary of English Etymology, means a 'disposition' which David Thomas, in his book *The Experience of Handicap* (1982), describes as an acquired orientation towards or away from some object, person, group, event or idea. While recognising both promotional and prejudicing aspects of an attitude, Thomas is optimistic that the dispositions involved are capable under certain circumstances of being modified or even reversed. If we accept this then it is a legitimate task to consider to what extent modifying or refocusing prejudicial attitudes towards the handicapped is part of the process of training teachers. We are, of course, caught somewhat in a dilemma here from the beginning. The very way we phrase our arguments, and in what direction, may arise from our own unconscious attitudes, whether they may be considered prejudicial or not. We cannot avoid this in attempting to examine this area of human functioning but we can be cognisant of whether we are consciously operating a prejudice by refusing to discuss the issues in the first place, and that is something we can do something about.

First a note on two terms which sometimes confuse by the juxtaposition in which they are used. It can be said that a person has a handicap with a consequent disablement. On the other hand the approach may be that we see children who consequently may or may not be handicapped in their education according to a variety of aspects which include both active management and attitudes of approach. A prime example of this is the integration of both partial and profoundly deaf children into mainstream education. For some of these children, with good oral communication and appropriate hearing aids, the handicapping condition is not *per se* that of deafness while the child is in school. The handicap may well arise from how the child is managed, i.e. segregated from others which may constitute the handicap.

Society and Attitude Change

There may be an overall impression that there has been a marked change in society's attitude towards those with disabilities. This change has been referred to as a social revolution in which their status has altered from discrimination to derogation through custodial and philanthropic concerns, and on towards the goal of integration (Thomas 1978). Reports such as Court (1976) and the Snowdon Working Party (1976) may be viewed as examples of attempts to establish structural social changes which aim to remove physical, economic and social barriers. Warnock (1979) perceived the relevance of her Report (1978) as not only to bring about a general framework within which educational provision could be made for those disabled, but also to reflect and change attitudes:

> The effect on attitudes comes about through the actual publication of the Report, the immense amount of thought that goes into the preparation of evidence, and the posthumous discussion before any White Paper appears.

Alongside the basic structure of legislation, housing, jobs, care, which increasingly involves central and local government, researchers draw attention to the phenomena of growing involvement of concerned people, expressing their wish to help the disabled, either through voluntary services or simply as individuals (Cope and Anderson, 1977). If special education is a matter for the nation, communities, institutions and individuals (Sabatino, 1972) we are also pointedly reminded that every one of us is in some way disabled or likely to become so with the attrition of years (Snowdon Working Party, 1976).

If in America it can be said that much of the support for integration (mainstreaming) has evolved from the concerns of society in general, then this finds a reflection in the new heroes of special education who appear to be lawyers, judges and legislators, rather than educators. (Blatt, 1972). It might be argued that in Britain the same legal toe-hold has been established by nature of the 1981 Education Act, although there is much scepticism about this (Swann et al., 1984). But herein lies a paradox. The 1981 Education Act sustains the distinction between two groups in educational society, those 'statemented' and those, so called normal children, who are 'non-statemented'. The language has changed over time from abnormal and normal to special and ordinary and now to statemented and non-statemented (Jones, 1985). There is no shift here in society's attitude as expressed in legislation towards those who in some respect are different and are set apart. The evidence supports the contention that whilst individuals - usually heads of particular special and ordinary schools - have moved to accommodate less prejudicial views about how children should be educated (Booth and Potts, 1983) the statistics show that as a consequence of the 1981 Act the major increase in response has been a ten per cent increase in special education administrators, advisers and services. Special schools continue to be filled and new ones are opened. None of these developments ensures that a single additional child becomes a member of normal society attending a normal school. If a resource element is required it will be for enhanced teacher staffing and not additional bureaucracy. There is little doubt, as Warnock said, that the debate since 1978 has been strong, but following the enactment of the 1981 Education Act completely time-consuming for many professionals. The evidence for a move from old attitudes lies not only in the thinking, which may constitute little more than the re-arranging of mental prejudices, but in the observable changes; and these are still somewhat peripheral (Jones, 1983).

Attitudes Towards Disability

First let us look at the nature of disability. The layman is likely to think of disability in its physical sense where there is some loss of function or capacity. The extent to which a disability becomes handicapping depends on its severity and nature, its prognosis and amenability to treatment, the extent to which it interferes with everyday life, and the attitudes of other people to it. Furthermore, the extent to which a disability is a handicap also depends on the personal meaning the loss of function has for an individual (Thomas, 1978). The handicapping element in any disability is, it appears, the psychological overtones which the disability engenders.

Meyerson (1956) has argued that both terms 'disability' and 'handicap' are judgements that are made relative to social values. In this sense physical disability is not concerned with functional limitation alone but has social and psychological consequences that stem from the reaction of others to the disabled person and that person's needs for dependence (Hewitt, 1970; Booth 1982). The combination of these, in degree and variety, are the rule rather than the exception. Barker and his colleagues (1953) enter a caveat about the dangers of viewing all physically disabled persons as being a homogeneous group psychologically: physique is only one factor in an extensive context of environmental conditions acting together to create the particular life situations of the person. The view has been put forward that each disability label or description evokes its own set of attitudes and stereotypes and the establishment of social distance varies according to the type and severity of the impairment (Jaffe, 1967). Negative attitudes and evaluations may be more related to the *condition* of disability *per se* with blindness arousing very special attitudes reserved for the blind. Four-year-old children are thought to be able to perceive that they have limitations which are imposed upon them by the physical disabilities (Jones, 1966) and children with cerebral palsy appear to suffer more rejection than children with other forms of handicap (Cope and Anderson, 1977). The underlying issue appears to be whether there is likely to be a close relationship or not: children with physical disabilities seem to be discriminated against more than children with sensory disablements as this applies to being a friend, co-worker, playmate or marriage partner.

The attitude of the public towards disability would seem to vary according to the perception made as to its nature, severity and prognosis, as well as according to age. Disabled children appear to suffer less than adults as reflected in personal encounters as well as discrimination implicit in legal or administrative restraints. Social relationship between the disabled and non-disabled develops in three characteristic stages (Davis, 1964). First, there are the norms of behaviour for a given social group and these cultural factors operate so that we behave to the disabled person equally as we would to any other member of the social group. This in reality is a 'fictional' acceptance of the disability and in essence the relationship is starved and kept at a bare substance. A second stage is where the personal characteristics of the disabled person ceases to be aware of the functional impairment. The third stage is where the non-disabled person is aware of the functional impairment and takes it into account but does not allow it to interfere with the social relationship.

A training objective for ordinary teachers might well encompass this notion of three-stage interaction by a process of self monitoring of their own perceptions and feelings in the teaching of a child who is severely disabled. It is likely that the model is not as precise as indicated by Davis and that for every individual teacher there will be indivualised responses that will be triggering off a range of conscious and unconscious feelings and reactions. To cope with this there must, therefore, be a context whereby a student can express and explore sensitively those deep rooted feelings and what may be personal antagonisms and conflicts and that context must be firmly located in the training process. The essence of this aspect of training is its reality component where real feelings and attitudes are being expressed and evaluated.

This does not prevent, however, the simulated style of learning illustrated in a number of American studies. One of the difficulties in determining what attitudes create a response in individual student teachers is the fact that different stimuli evoke different responses. Investigations have been wide and varied to investigate this phenomenon. Some researchers have used photographs, written descriptions of disabled persons, actual persons and labels such as 'mentally retarded', 'neurotic', 'cripple' and disabled person' (Mussen and Barker, 1964).

Teacher Perceptions

Research in ordinary schools can throw light on the extent to which there is confusion in the minds of teachers about children with disabilities and reflects to some extent the way and degree this area has been handled, if at all, in teacher training. So often it is regarded as something that the teacher is unlikely to come across on an assumption that ordinary teachers do not concern themselves with disabled children nor are they, certainly by secondary age, likely to be met with in ordinary schools. This, of course, tends to break down in relation to the two largest groups of children with disabilities, the slow learner and the maladjusted, because these problems tend to emerge as children progress through their school years. Hence every ordinary teacher will at some time encounter such children unless there has been a fierce exclusion programme, either to exclude the child totally or to set the child apart in specially designated classes or units.

In spite of this, confusions persist: this may take the form of confusion between retardation and backwardness. A distinction is not made between the child of normal intelligence who may in some respect be retarded in basic subjects like reading and arithmetic, and the slow-learning child whose level of functioning in some areas may simply be due to low cognitive skills. This situation becomes further complicated if a child's responses are slowed up as a result of drug sedation aimed at controlling epileptic fits. Secondly, the terms 'disability' and 'handicap' are often used synonymously and little thought is given to whether a child's disability necessarily implies handicap in school. Too often a straight correlation is made between disability and some extra resource without there first being some thought about the actual handicapping conditions that may pertain. There needs to be a searching out of ways to minimise the handicapping conditions in the school; this may simply apply to how, for example, a child in a wheelchair gets around the school, copes in a physics lab or a woodwork room, and the location in the school of certain lessons that do not allow for easy access by wheelchairs. All this involves an orientation and attitude towards what is, and what is not, the task of teachers when a school makes a response to its child population that is more 'whole school' or 'community' orientated than when segregationist views pertain.

A third area is confusion about maladjustment. Some view this as maladaptive behaviour developed over the years to compensate for the lack of basic needs being met in early childhood (Pringle 1974). Concerned as part of the matrix of psychiatric disorders where the maladjustment is 'severe, complex and persisting' then the disorder is defined as marked and prolonged abnormalities of behaviour, emotions or relationships, sufficient to give rise to handicap which might affect the family, community or child herself (Rutter et al., 1970). Neither of these explanations help teachers in their work with problem children because they both point towards causes outside the present classroom situation. They do not help the teacher to understand the feelings that problem children are capable of arousing, what attitudes should be taken towards the disruption involved, and what action is required. What is involved in all situations relating to maladjustment in schools are two people (teacher and child) and a context (usually the class group).

A starting point teachers may well consider is whether there are adjustment problems as between the child's skills and abilities (and these are not only academic but how well a child can cope emotionally and socially) and the demands made or expectations raised of the child's environment. This ecological approach locates the disturbance in the interaction between a child and critical aspects of that child's system (Apter S, 1982). Maladjustment perceived in these terms locates the issue securely as between child and teacher and enables a first appraisal to be made by the teacher. But what determines whether a teacher will want to embark on such a line of questioning? This surely relates to whether teachers feel that it is their task to do so (and not all teachers accept this), whether the teachers are secure in their own skills to ensure that they are not becoming enmeshed in issues far beyond the tasks required for classroom work (and this implies a network of reference, support and consultation within the school staff), and whether teachers have the personal skills to extend this part of their pastoral role. There are so many 'oughts' here which are built around these issues and the one place the teacher should not attempt to resolve them is in the actual context of confrontation with a child, but so often this is what happens in practice. Attitudes therefore to abnormal or deviant behaviour, and the teacher's response to this, are clearly part of any teaching objective at the training level. This becomes more pertinent if it is accepted that disruption arises not only as a function of mismatch between a child and the immediate environment, ie. in the given learning situation in the classroom, but embraces wider management and structural elements in the way the life of a school is organised and run (Tattum, 1982). Here the teacher is concerned, not only with a minority who disrupt, but with all children in the school whose learning and development are impinged upon by structural considerations. It may be the case that given inappropriate structures for living and learning it is the disruptive phenomena in a school which highlight this and act as a temperature gauge for when life in a school is just too hot for all concerned. Here again there can be confusion. One school with appropriate objectives may simply be unable to carry these out satisfactorily and hence will experience disruption in an overt way. Another school, however, may set its levels so low that there is never a challenge and little expectation for children to learn so that accommodation is the keynote throughout. Teachers in training need to look at styles of management within school which arise from attitudes towards a whole spectrum of issues in education, and to find out what for them individually is their own 'style' of being a teacher. So often this emerges after a teacher has been appointed to a particular school.

Teacher Attitudes and Hierarchies

Mittler (1979) drew attention to the fact that research in special education had yielded little that would help policy makers but that all studies identify one phenomenon, that of teacher behaviour and teacher attitudes. Although teacher attitudes in general are basic to their performance in the classroom, it would be unwise to hypothesise about these attitudes where disability is concerned. Cope and Anderson (1977) found that teacher responses depended on the amount of support they could call upon if they were asked to teach a disabled child; and secondly, whether the teachers had any actual experience they could draw upon. The prospect of having a disabled child in one's class seemed to be more worrying than the reality. A case is often made that before a disabled child joins an ordinary school there should be wide ranging discussions with the teachers concerned. Experience teaches, however, that the effect of this is only to heighten teacher anxiety and so the placement becomes null and void as some form of rationalisation takes over. Sometimes this can be as general as, on principle (though whose principle it is never clear), no disabled child should be placed in the ordinary school without resources. What is needed is for some limited discussion to take place but with a guarantee that if over a period of time the placement is failing then the child will be removed. Some may argue that this sets up the expectation for failure and guarantees exclusion but practice does not bear this out. In reality the disabled child soon loses its 'disability mantle' and becomes 'Jane' or 'Fred' to whom other children and the staff relate. Seldom is the problem the disability as such but increases so if additional to the disability are associated problems of severe learning difficulties and particularly maladjustment.

Garnett (1976) found in her study of the evolution of a special unit in a comprehensive school that the motivating influence for change came from staff questioning why particular children should be segregated out in the unit. These children were slow-learners but because they were part of the pupil role of the school, part of the inter-relatedness of relationships, they were also part of the care and concern of the school and were influenced by the ethos of the school. This would not have happened, and does not happen, when children are placed elsewhere in special units and schools, where they stay out of sight and out of mind.

The studies of Rutter (1979) and Bandura (1969) reiterate that standards of behaviour in schools are those that are set in the first place by the staff. Children not only copy specific behaviour but they tend to identify in a more general way with the people whom they follow and come to adopt what they perceive to be their values and attitudes. This pattern of behaviour of teacher to child extends also to teacher and teacher, and from this arises that ubiquitous phenomenon, the school ethos, which Measor and Woods (1984) regard as 'not a thing, nor a settled state of affairs with constant parameters to which all subscribe in equal measure... but a moving set of relationships within which different groups and individuals are constantly in negotiation'. It is difficult to envisage the special groups in some comprehensive schools, located in special classes for slow learners for the whole of their secondary schooling, engaging in 'constant negotiation' with others, but of course, these groups are expressions of attitudes institutionalised in organisational and curriculum terms.

Teacher attitudes, and acceptability of disablement in the classroom, are related to a certain kind of experience which in itself derives from opportunities to meet, teach, learn about the needs of the disabled, and to reflect on one's own reponses to these experiences. An objective for the teaching and training of students might well lie therefore in being provided with opportunities to engage in the experience of teaching the disabled. This, however, encompasses yet another attitude within the teaching fraternity itself which is derived

from how individual teachers appraise their professional status
as among their professional peers. Westwood (1967) has
suggested that status within the educational framework is
determined by the age of the pupils taught, their ability, and
the type of school in which they are taught. Teachers of
secondary school children enjoy a higher status than those
teaching in primary schools: teachers in grammar schools were
more highly regarded than those in either of the other two.
Whatever the truth in this, and it could well have some
credence, it reminds us that attitudes that have a
discriminatory flavour are not preserved only for those with
disabilities. It may well be asked why it is that amongst
teachers as a professional group there are such strong
boundaries drawn around particular teacher groups, i.e.nursery,
primary, secondary, and further education, and why these groups
so tenaciously cling to their individual professional
affiliations. Even heads have a pecking order. When applied
to groups of children with disabilities there is evidence to
suggest that teachers within special education enjoy a status
according to the kind of disability they specialise in teaching
(Jones and Gottfried, 1966).

There is little doubt that certain groups in society, even
among the disabled, enjoy a 'status' that can in some respect
be related to some hierarchical structure of preference where
teachers have a choice. A number of studies have been carried
out concerning attitudes towards specific handicaps showing
that there is amongst teachers a clear preference, but it is
difficult to know how such preferences can fit into a teacher's
commitment to individualised learning and the recognition of
individual differences. There are clearly cut-off points when
a child's disability becomes more than can be coped with by an
individual teacher so these children become part of the
category of children seen as 'difficult to teach'. But may it
not be the case that historically a class has become associated
with a given number of children, all of whom are within a given
range of intellectual ability, and the majority of the same
age? The teacher in practice teaches to the norm so that
deviance, defined as different to the norm and a certain
statistical distribution, by definition has to be excluded.
This is decided by a cut-off point of IQ rating for the slow
learner, a medical classification for the physically disabled,
and by a behavioural questionnaire for the maladjusted child.
These cut-off points vary according to different disabilities
but it would be useful to know whether it has been the system
described above that has established the hierarchy of attitudes
or whether attitudes expressed in operational terms of the
number of children and their varying problems have dictated the
attitudes. What is not clear is whether attitudes, even in
hierarchies, represent specific choices or whether there is
really an across-the-board attitude of discrimination to all

disability and this finds individual expression as related to individual teacher's circumstance.

Attitudes and Training

Students are not the custodians of attitudes towards the disabled, whether prejudicial or not: tutors also have attitudes. One reflection of this is in the type of course that is designed by tutors especially in the area of special education. Some courses simply teach the 'system' and this means that students are introduced to the categories of disability and the ways in which there has been a response to these within state education. On such courses students may visit special schools to see how the 'system' works and may even join for a day or two some of the gate-keepers of the system, e.g. the school doctors or educational psychologists. If the student is going to work in the system then the training and experience is likely to be appropriate. The ACSET Committee Report of 1984 has, however, come down hard on those training courses that take student teachers in green and without having had training and experience in the teaching of ordinary children. With more disabled children being retained in ordinary schools these teachers, special from the beginning, are in one sense de-skilled by their lack of training and experience in ordinary schools and become a professionally isolated group among the teaching fraternity.

A second type of course is where the levels of the segregation system are taught to teachers who already work in ordinary schools and who will return to ordinary schools at the end of their training course. In general, such teachers enjoy seeing the other side of the fence and visiting special schools to see mongols in action with their behavioural objectives curriculum.

A third type of course, which is difficult to find, tackles the problems of teaching disabled children in normal contexts. Here the issues relate to attitudes on the part of subject teachers, to actual classroom organisation and management, to re-evaluating expectations and living with children whose style of learning, pace and level may be different from what most teachers are taught to expect to find in the so-called normal school.

The reason why it is so difficult to find courses of the third type is because of the shortage of tutors to teach on them. As soon as a course is designated 'special' then it is assumed that the expertise will be provided, has to be provided, not by those familiar in working with disabled pupils in ordinary schools, but with those with a background training and experience in special education in special schools. This is not to denigrate those who run and organise courses on special education for teachers in ordinary schools but to highlight a management issue that has national as well as local LEA implications. A quick look at the syllabus of these courses will show that most of the topic work is about education in 'special' environments, that practical course work is related to visits and projects linked to special schools and units, and that outside visiting speakers will invariably be those whose expertise lies in the special system. Unless there is a change of attitude that permeates from the Department of Education and Science through LEAs and universities, and finds a reflection in street-level organisation and management, then we shall continue to find that the heads and teachers of ordinary schools, where the disabled will receive their education, will continue to be an excluded group as amongst tutors and trainers.

These problems are particularly compounded in handicap awareness courses organised by LEAs through their special advisory services (Jones and Jones, 1981). Such courses have a useful but limited life if they are to achieve their aims in terms of making teachers aware. But much of the material required to create this knowledge of awareness can just as effectively be made available within schools as part of in-service training. To do this requires the advisory services to ordinary schools to take up this activity propagating the notion that what is being offered is part of normal teacher skills and knowledge. But where are the ordinary advisers who first regard this as a legitimate part of their work, and secondly, are prepared to promote it? Inevitably there is a fall back on those whose job it is to work in the special arena. Furthermore, teachers soon discover that they know more about the 'facts' of disability than they first realise. Once engaged, however, by interest or commitment, the urgency is for a different kind of knowledge and skills related to educating those children whose educational needs may be somehow different from that of the average child.

Just Attitudes

Perhaps it is appropriate to recall the passage from John Donne's *Devotions upon Emergent Occasions* published in 1621:

> No man is an island, intire of itself; every man is a peece of Continent, a part of the Maine, if a Clod bee washed away by the Sea, Europe is the less, as well as if a Mannor of thy friends or of theire owne were; any man's death diminishes me, because I am involved in Mankinde; And therefore never send to know for whom the bell tolls; it tolls for thee.

For some there is the belief that the transferring of 40,000 severely mentally disabled children from health departments to local education authorities in 1970 was an emergent occasion. Or was it a slip in the 'system' whereby the historical process of management from school doctor to school psychologist found reflection in a system that changed from special training to special education? Eleven years later, in Oxfordshire, the head of a special school for such children had what Mary Warnock once described as "a special imagination" and seven of his children were integrated into the local primary school. The following year eight more children followed to constitute a second class. In 1983 these children could move on to their 'normal' comprehensive school, where a class for secondary age children had been opened. What was beginning to develop was a new concept of special school, not so much a building, but a network of expertise and provision cast across a geographical community. It had taken nearly three years for this change to come about, reflecting new attitudes towards the disabled: this is the same time it takes to build a new special school where the reflected attitude to the disabled stretches back to antiquity. But how long can the disabled go on depending on some one person's imagination, and in spite of the formidable forces opposing the development of an education system geared to the needs and interests of all participants in it (Booth et al, 1982), when can the 'system' itself be generating its own progress? It seems likely that what is required is not so much a revolution in bricks and mortar so much as a speeded up evolution in ideas. There is now a growing literature on how things are and how they came about; no longer can we hide behind the excuse of not knowing what they could be in the future. There is little doubt that the barriers against change, while strongly posited in how society has responded to the disabled in the past, are never so strong as when they are rooted in strongly held beliefs and these in turn are upheld by attitudes which in some respect encompass the whole of our corporate lives. Attitudes can often be changed by example but this assumes sufficient example to emulate and a willingness to be a participant learner. It is, therefore, at the time when young teachers have chosen to become participant learners that there is the greatest opportunity for them to explore new emergent ways of embracing their chosen profession, that of teaching children, disabled or not.

Chapter Three

PATTERNS OF DELIVERY AND IMPLICATIONS FOR TRAINING

Denis Mongon

It is easy to believe that the Warnock Report and the 1981
Education Act are the only notable sources of change in
special education. They dominate current thinking and it is
impossible to attend a special education conference or
meeting without having to ask or answer, 'What are we/they
doing about Warnock and/or the Act?'. These preoccupations
are having some curious effects. First they obscure
fundamental questions about the origins of the Warnock Report
and the subsequent legislation - what pressures created them
and what constraints sculptured them?   Secondly, frequent
emphasis on what specialists are or should be doing causes a
sort of concave reflection, introverted and inverted, of the
relationship between special and mainstream provision. Both
these effects obscure the indissoluble connections between
'special' and 'mainstream'.   Warnock and the Act are not
about special education alone; taken seriously they are very
much about the organisation and quality of all schooling.
Similarly, 16+ exams, falling rolls, financial constraints,
youth unemployment, nursery provision and other ostensibly
mainstream concerns will have eventual albeit unpredictable
consequences on educational definitions of 'special'.

Nevertheless it is Warnock and the 1981 Act which are
providing a focus for attention on special education and it
is their perceived consequences which have created an
expectation of change for the 'service delivery model'.   If
any change does occur, teachers will need the experience and
skills to implement the new form of service; and the
introduction of relevant experience and skills into teacher
training requires a forward planning prediction of what the
new model will be. What follows is an attempt to consider
how such a prediction can be made.

Apparently the main impetus for change derives from the search for an educationally and philosophically sound approach to what are now called special educational needs. They are also sometimes called disabilities or handicaps although persistence of the notion that disability, handicap and need are synonymous only reflects how far the search has still to go. So far the search has culminated in a government enquiry, (Warnock), and the legislation, (the 1981 Act) which was said by members of the then government to be the statutory endorsement of the Warnock Report. There are less kindly interpretations of its purposes but on the face of things this pursuit of the best available models is a Good Thing. Yet all this activity disguises a less philanthropic reality in which education policy is not divined from ethereal and goodly manifestos - instead it marks the line of least resistance between forces manipulated by governments, professionals, parents and pressure groups representing these and other interests. It is important to understand that no aspect of policy creation is free from such pressures, not the Warnock Report, not the rhetoric which followed its publication, not the 1981 Act, not the decisions of LEAs and their employees about procedures, provision or placement and not the activity of parents or their representatives in the pursuit of consumer rights.

Predicting the form of the service delivery model is largely a question of making guesses - more or less well informed - about the stability, persistence and strength of the identifiable pressures and their eventual outcomes. Since Warnock and the Act are considered to be outstanding factors, it is worth asking for what particular sorts of change they are catalysts.

At best, Committees of Enquiry have a mixed reputation for producing official action:

> 'Bureaucratic delay, inadequate funding, a lack of coordination between central and local government, Ministers or Cabinets with a different set of priorities, internal politicking in Civil Service or Parties, a preference for elitist concerns instead of everyday ones - the reasons for lack of achievement are familiar.' (Rogers, 1984)

But surely these charges cannot be made to stick, for Warnock was well received; it did point a clear, generally acceptable way forward and has resulted in the 1981 Act and subsequent Regulations. The special education service is on the move - isn't it? Well, setting aside the argument about Warnock's reception and general acceptance (see Lewis et.

al., 1981), one way of evaluating progress would be to consider the fate of the Report's priority recommendations which were:

1.   Provision for children under five with special educational needs.
2.   Provision for young people over sixteen with special needs.
3.   Teacher training.

Notwithstanding the parental involvement written into the Act, it is difficult to identify a government initiative which responds to the first priority. On the contrary, the evidence is that the steady proportionate increase in under fives attending maintained schools ground to a halt at the start of the 1980s, (Education 1984); and the shortcomings identified by HMI (DES 1983) offer no scope for optimism in this field.

Government activity on 16+ education has been mostly confined to minimal parliamentary answers acknowledging the duty of LEAs to make provision for:

> '... any young person under the age of 19 who wishes to continue full time education,' (Hansard 1982)

Although ministers refused to circulate a reminder of that duty on the presumption that LEAs were already aware of it, parents were finding that LEAs could describe this as a legislative 'grey area' or even deny any legal responsibility, (G.L.A.D. 1984). It is only after considerable pressure group campaigning (ibid) that the government has agreed to issue a circular reminding LEAs of the existing law.

Teacher training for special educational needs has been considered by the Advisory Committee on the Supply and Education of Teachers which has made a variety of recommendations to the Secretary of State. The first reaction in the news media has not been in terms of general principles, but from interest groups, whose spheres of influence and expertise may be affected. Under the auspices of Circular 3/83 and more recently Circular 4/84 the DES has provided funds to enable teachers to be seconded on to one-term courses 'intended for teachers who have, or may be taking up, responsibility for children with special educational needs in primary and secondary schools'. The funds amounted to about one million pounds for the first year and have been increased in the second year. Whatever the value of the courses for individual students even at double the rate of initial funding it would take half a century for each primary and secondary school to be represented on the courses.

It is quite clear that Warnock's three priority areas have been neglected perhaps because the funds which Warnock herself thought would be necessary and available (Hansard 1981) have not been forthcoming. A small point should also be made about 'Integration' which was never an explicit priority of the Report although it is often talked about in that way. This view is so well established that it might be expected to have had some effect on practice yet between 1978 and 1983 the proportion of children in special schools in England showed a slight increase! (DES 1978. 1983)

What then can one expect of the 1981 Act? After a year or so of operation its main outcome seems to have been 'more to do with administration than with education' (NARE, 1984). This is largely because of what have been called 'time-consuming and costly procedures of assessing and making statements' (Peter, 1984). These, Peter argues, combine with financial constraints to ensure that the Act's wider intentions go unmet. The Act's wider intentions are of course arguable, but presumably the reference is to Section 2 of the Act which outlines the limited obligation on LEAs to secure that children for whom they maintain a statement are educated in ordinary schools. Such are the limits on that obligation, (Sections 2.3.b and c refer to 'efficient education for the children with whom he will be educated' and 'efficient use of resources') that even if LEAs made this part of the Act their first and absolute priority they would each still be able to develop their service in the way which suited their political or fiscal ambitions. Until this matter comes before the courts for judicial interpretation, and perhaps even after that, there is no particular form of service delivery for which the Act is either sufficient or necessary.

None of this elementary questioning of the real impact of Warnock and the Act can obscure the considerable huffing and puffing which now preoccupies the special education services. A great deal of this, it has just been noted, is directed at understanding the statutory assessment procedures, reorganising services to meet those statutory features and then coming to terms with the subsequent imbroglio. But there is also now a communal awareness - or more correctly, supposition - within LEAs and schools that a notional two per cent of their pupils have severe and complex needs while as many as a notional eighteen per cent may require some form of special help sometime during their school career. These figures show signs of being elevated to the mythology of education statistics even though they were never Warnock's precise figures and despite the Report's proviso that proportions inevitably vary. How then should these different groups be identified, assessed and catered for? Mainstream schools are scrutinising their curricula and organisation, the role of the 'remedial department' being the subject of particular interest. Special schools, some with an understandably anxious eye on falling rolls, are re-examining both their internal curricula and their external relationships with other schools and agencies. Surely all this activity must be leading to changes in the service delivery model?

One answer to that must be 'yes' because things are unlikely to look the same once so much dust is allowed to settle, but there must be a query about the depth of change, which may only be cosmetic. Warnock's enduring commitment was to psychological and medical perspectives which inevitably end in an individual focus; the 1981 Act was concerned to preach against sin without paying the price of redemption. As a result of that there are mirages of innovation, the proximity of which tantalises or threatens according to interpretation. There is no clear impulse to which the service could not respond nor a clear path for it to follow.

It is in that kind of vacuum that other pressures can have greatest effect and in this context none more so than the paramountcy of the fourth and fifth year secondary school curriculum. That phenomenon which is sustained by its own historical rationale permeates lower secondary and primary school classrooms. It encourages the hierarchical, stratified schooling in which status and resources consistently drift away from the children about whom this paper is concerned. To compensate for that, a 'special education' service will still have to be grafted on to the mainstream element and as long as it has to be grafted on then it will be regarded as intrinsically separate and specialist. In turn, as long as special provision is regarded in that light then integrative changes will be essentially superficial.

Warnock's notional twenty per cent is not a small tail wagging the dog, it is a substantial proportion of the school population. If our present schooling does not adequately meet the needs of so many children, then it is an odd use of language to call those needs 'special'. There is a sense, naturally, in which all children have special needs and Warnock herself has expressed misgivings about the term 'special educational needs' for whose ubiquity her Report is largely responsible (1983a). That is not the point; we tolerate an education service whose general provision is arguably unsatisfactory for as many as twenty per cent of its students and whose dominant exam syllabi are commonly described as unsuitable for about forty per cent. These are large numbers and to describe the unmet needs of the former twenty per cent as 'special' is potentially misleading.

Acceptance of that misleading element reflects a common inability to grasp and explore the philosophical basis from which the education of this group should proceed. Most of us have a long experience stretching back into our childhoods of being told and believing that disabled and profoundly disadvantaged people were best helped by being clearly identified and provided for in compensatory specialist institutions - a way of looking at things which extended to the tripartite division of secondary education. This fixed in our minds the notion that particular groups are different or special, that the differences between us and them override the similarities and that integration means doing something for or to them. The shift away from medical language, the publication of critical research and literature, changes in the pattern of schooling and consumer advocacy now oblige us to think again.

The commitment to comprehensive schooling is well established in the maintained primary sector. In the secondary sector it is occasionally diminished by leaks into selective and/or independent schools, but its popularity has been demonstrated by the parental response to recent LEA attempts to reintroduce or expand selective schooling. If comprehensive schooling means anything in terms of special educational needs, it cannot be that there is an identifiable, discrete group of children for or to whom the schools should do something *intrinsically* different, i.e. special. After all, one expression of the comprehensive ideal is the end of special schooling for children whose IQ score exceeded the median by one or more standard deviations. The central issue for schools addressing the intrinsically common features of their pupils' learning should not be to create a curricular plan which accommodates a particular form of streaming, banding or grouping. Instead each school's organisation should reflect curricular decisions made in the light of all their pupils educational needs.

There is a paragraph (1.4) in the Warnock Report which says with added detail that the purpose of education, the goals, are the same for all children. In similar vein David Aspin wrote:

> '....autonomy, enrichment, the capacity to come to terms with the world and to make it a suitable vehicle for the promotion of our own happiness ... these are educational goals which we set up for

any and every child' (1982)

Such statements about the aims of education seem to be much the same and quite uncontentious for all children. There is great disagreement about how to translate them into workable curricular objectives and processes. Yet children who are said to have special educational needs do not learn in fundamentally different ways to other children: intrinsic and extrinsic rewards, relevance, importance, motivation, habits of thinking, knowledge of results and so on are as important to these children as they are to me or anyone else. At the same time, teachers have the responsibility of organising experiences so that the pupils' learning techniques are best deployed and that is similarly achieved for all pupils: familiar bases, attainable objectives, the use of analogy, guided discovery, the prevalence of clear, sound planning, and so on.

The central elements of the pupils' and teachers' rôles are therefore things that they *do*, the *activities* of school life. They are features of the curriculum process, and yet schools persist in conceiving and presenting their curricular plans in terms of their *content*. This reinforces the hierarchical and status allocation of knowledge and neglects the need for effective learning skills to be both the purpose and the vehicle of curricular activity. It is less important to know whether a school's curriculum encompasses the Battle of Hastings than to know how historical material is dealt with. If then some children have difficulty in learning it is as possible and important to think about what should be done to the curricular processes as what should be done for those discrete groups.

Where does that take us in terms of a service delivery model and its implications for teacher training? Three important points have emerged: firstly that changes in the education service are never free from and are sometimes the product of conflicting pressures; secondly neither the Warnock Report nor the 1981 Act provides a sufficient rationale for change; finally principles of what is called 'integration' are concerned not only with special education but are fundamentally bound to the ethic of comprehensive schooling. The points are simple enough in themselves; they are not a revelation, but they do pose interesting questions about the role of teacher training. Training can no longer be seen as the vacuous apolitical response to service delivery models - it becomes an active agent in the creation of models. Consequently, training for a new service delivery model is not only a matter of enhancing delivery skills but must also be concerned with the reasons teachers have for developing or supporting new models. Such training would continue to provide knowledge and techniques in areas like communication with the deaf, technological aids for the blind, the symptomatology of physical handicap and so on; those *content* elements would be unchanged. In terms of how that service should be delivered to pupils, which is of course a *processual* element, training should become less dependent on central guidance and more responsive to demands made by groups of teachers. The model for good teacher-learning - and I shall return again to this point - is no different to that for good pupil-learning, so it is essential for training to identify with the concerns of the trainees. In the case of in-service training that means developing from the experience and preoccupations of interested teachers. It is unlikely that they are seeking or could adequately profit from exposure to theoretical perspectives which they are then expected to carry out into practice. It should be possible and more profitable to allow teachers to share and contextualise their experiences so they develop a theoretical perspective which illuminates and enhances their own work. At this point in a teacher's career theory should be derived from practice not blindly directing it.

This does raise one other issue - whether the word 'training' properly describes the process which would then be going on. 'Training' carries the connotation of activity carried out under the close supervision of an instructor who has set the goals by which efficiency will be judged. This could hardly be the case with a model in which teachers took far greater responsibility for defining the purpose and manner of the exercise. Maybe the analogy with pupils' learning should be extended so that much as we prefer the term 'education' rather than 'training' to describe what happens in schools maybe the same could apply to those occasions when teachers seek help with their own learning.

Classroom Based Service

Although special educational needs are currently attracting the kind of bandwagon interest which has some of us recalling the heady days of Bullock, that may not last. There is a confusion of messages from 'the top' which suggests that the protection of 'standards' is thought of more in terms of getting as many pupils through traditional examinable content-loaded syllabi than in enhancing the educational experience of those who are already failed by that approach. If that view prevails, then schooling will continue to be dominated by notions of 'pass and fail' which inevitably damn a notable proportion of children. The alternative is to endow the teaching force and the education community with an awareness that standards are not synonymous with '...the ability to memorise large amounts of material even if they (pupils) haven't understood it' - a common measure of school success, (DES, 1984). That means looking more carefully at (or for) the strategies which best meet all educational needs and which enable all children's learning to be most effective.

Institutions concerned with the education of teachers will probably argue that they already do what the previous paragraph asks but a great deal - if not most - teacher socialisation takes place informally in schools. This hegemony of the staffroom has varied consequences for pupils (Rutter, 1979, Reynolds, 1981) and for attitudes to handicap (Hegarty, 1982). It must therefore be a persuasive and durable message in all teacher education that the skills and ideas which are available are applicable to the schooling of all pupils. If the hidden curriculum of teachers' own education is that twenty per cent of pupils have special needs which must be dealt with in another specialist course or in specialist elements of courses, then it is impossible to see how the ideal of comprehensive schooling can be sustained through that kind of teaching development. Unless the sense of responsibility for all pupils permeates teacher education,teachers will be unable to answer 'Why?' questions about the structure of schools and the context of their work. Without convincing answers to those questions they cannot progress to answer 'What' questions about content and process in their curricular design - except in a shoddy pragmatic fashion, the inheritance of stale ideas and structures.

There is a phrase enjoying current vogue which runs something like 'every teacher a special needs teacher'. I justify my own daily use of it on heuristic grounds but it is not in the final analysis a sufficient perspective. Its value is in providing a shorthand pointer to the truism that whatever label is used to describe the group, ('the 20%', 'SEN pupils', 'children whose access to the curriculum is obstructed' and so on), the overwhelmingly vast majority of its members will have their formal education provided in 'ordinary' classrooms by 'ordinary' teachers. This is the unmistakably dominant feature of old or new service delivery models yet one which can be overlooked amidst the higher status scramble to create 'specialisms'.

Consequently at the end of initial or INSET courses it will not be enough for teachers to be satisfactory mainstream practitioners whose new insight into special needs is an appendage to their daily strategies and activities. Instead they should know how they intend to meet hitherto unmet needs and feel a sense of their own competence and responsibility for meeting them. This is a reversal of the previous deskilling of teachers which led them to believe that only specialists can help children with special needs and that their own pedagogic skills are irrelevant. A teaching force which grasps the endemic features of learning and teaching will be able to respond to the variations in pace and style which occur not just between pupils but also within individuals and from time to time and in different contexts. It would in the end enable schools to cater for all their comprehensive intake and change the trajectory which marks the line of least resistance between the pressure impinging on the service delivery model.

There is no presumption in this approach that initial courses will be able to equip teachers to meet single-handed the needs of any and every child they encounter. On the contrary, children's education should be a collaborative enterprise, or more ideally a partnership, between a number of participants. Partnership cannot be taken for granted between professionals, parents and pupils. Yet even amongst themselves teachers continue to suffer from the 'deep sea diver syndrome': although serviced by modern executives and supported by advanced technology they sink or swim on their own, isolates in a potentially hostile environment. Here is another major concern for all teacher training, because if the full range of educational needs is to be met, then classrooms will have to be increasingly open to shared contributions and evaluation. This is not to say that every classroom needs an Adviser or 'line-manager' sitting in the back corner - far from it. It means that teachers should be able to invite their peers to share the planning, implementation and evaluation of classroom activity at a much more fundamental level than generally occurs at present. There are, of course, timetabling constraints on this kind of enterprise, especially in primary schools, but the greater difficulty is that many teachers feel too uncomfortable to request cooperation, even asking a friend to sit in and comment on a lesson can be threatening to both parties. This is not a natural phenomenon, most adults perform some of their work under the scrutiny of other adults. It is the professional de-socialisation of teachers which produces this quite different perspective.

Again the problem is striking for the close parallels which can be drawn between the needs in pupils' education and the needs of teacher education. In both, the prevalent model has been of atomised learning in which performance and achievement are measured individual against individual. Yet outside teaching and schooling it is more common for learning to occur or for skills and knowledge to be used when people are doing something together - solving a problem, completing a task or whatever. It follows that one of the goals of pupils' education should be the ability to cooperate in that kind of way and, as I have already said, the same ability is a desirable quality amongst teachers. Pupils and teachers will therefore require far more opportunity for collaborative work which presents a challenge to content, process and evaluation in schools and higher education but can also present a far wider range of profitable experience to the learners. It would be impossible for the kind of in-service model to which I referred earlier - responding to local requirements identified by groups of teachers - to avoid the development of collaborative ventures. In fact those ventures would be the normal formula for such in-service work. There may be some temptation to think that initial courses could still rely on a didactic approach but this would be incompatible with the ambition of encouraging new teachers to introduce their pupils to more ambitious collaborative problem-solving. I am suggesting that the most useful and effective learning occurs when teachers (in schools) and lecturers (in colleges) abandon the role of fountainhead-director and become harmonising-facilitator.

Supporting Services

The partnership which is created by collaborative work amongst teachers should be capable of embracing pupils and parents even if there are inevitable differences of opinion about what constitutes a fruitful partnership between teachers and the consumers. It should also encompass colleagues within the education service who represent the first line of response when teachers feel the need for assistance or advice.

The points made so far about the bedrock of comprehensive principles, about the universality of pedagogy and learning and about the importance of partnership are applicable to all teacher training. They should help to establish competence and confidence which will rearrange perspectives on educational need and reclassify 'special'. However, they cannot be a panacea and there will still need to be specialised support on the inevitable occasions when a sense of inadequacy or failure overwhelms pupils or teachers.

The importance of smooth communication and coherent planning between those different areas of service was emphasised during the USA Congressional hearings of P.L. 94-142:

> '...numerous individuals and advocacy group representatives testified that communication amongst and within service delivery agencies ... impaired the conversion of policies into practice ...' (O'Shea, 1983)

47

Initial teaching courses will have to sensitise teachers to both the range of specialist services available as well as to questions of knowing when and how to draw on those services. What the range might be is the subject of the following paragraphs.

i)   School Focused Services

Initially, that support must come from someone who is readily accessible, can spare the time and knows the context well.   That person in secondary schools could be in the academic or pastoral systems, or be located in a specialist department.   Primary schools may have an individual teacher who can perform this role but are more likely to pool some sort of peripatetic service.   Irrespective of the adopted model the first priority is for every teacher to understand how the local system works, which in turn requires a clearly understood and effective policy and structure.   This is essentially a management issue which will have to be encompassed on education management courses and on courses with a broader emphasis aimed at schools' management personnel.   Heads and deputy-heads in all schools, heads of year or heads of department in secondary schools and some post-holders in primary schools must be able to structure and direct a response to special needs within their sphere of influence.

That said, schools should also be able to call upon the specialist services of a teacher who can not only advise senior management on general strategy, or departments and staff on curricular development, but also provide a personal resource in the implementation of strategy, in the design of curricula and, if necessary, in the creation of programmes for individual pupils.   Coventry's 'SNAP' programme (Ainscow 1983, SNAP 1982) is one of the initiatives which explicitly encourage schools to nominate a member of staff for this role. In Coventry the title 'coordinator for special needs' is used to describe one designated teacher in each primary school; Norfolk, in another example, are using a similar title for one teacher in each secondary school.   In neither case is it necessary, or even possible, for every teacher concerned to have had previous 'special needs experience' - a clear portrayal of the common thread binding special and ordinary work which should not become an excuse for ignoring the in-service needs of the new post-holders.   In some large secondary schools the senior or deputy-head teacher may become the designated person but in many cases this role is often bestowed on the head of a 'born-again' remedial department rechristened 'special needs', 'learning support' or whatever.   The different history and internal structure of primary schools mean that they are more likely to use peripatetic or similar measures.

The five key aspects of this new role which were identified by the National Association for Remedial Education - Assessment, Prescription, Teaching/Therapeutic, Supportive and Liaison (NARE, 1979) - suggest that the staff involved are drawn into a kind of consultative role of which Heron and Harris wrote:

> 'The consultant can work individually with a student, a teacher, or administrator, to change their behaviour, or he can work indirectly with one of them to change the behaviour of a third party. Regardless, it is necessary for the consultant to have a clear idea of the problem to be solved, options for solving it, available resources, and evaluation techniques, prior to initiating the consultation.' (1982)

The main implication of this development is for a number of teachers to be able to adopt, retail and implement a general overview of the initial stages of indentification and response. The number involved is quite large - one in fifty teachers would mean a total approaching 10,000. The skills and knowledge required are largely an extension or refinement of those already available somewhere within the teachers' training or experience. They will therefore need to become better informed and more insightful about things of which they are already more or less fitfully aware. The constraints on current initial and in-service education leave no space for the reinforced general overview which is being suggested, though an exception occurs in the designated '3/83' courses to which an earlier reference was made. The notion of one term secondments - or equivalents - which create time for the consumption of a diet balanced between an 'academic' institution and the usual workplace could meet the above requirements. Peripheral support, before, during and following the secondment, from LEA support or advisory services would enhance the potential. ACSET is recommending to the Secretary of State that additional funding should be found for such courses. The success of this enterprise still depends on the release of funds by the Government and then on the ability of the organisers to design courses which productively balance coordination/organisation skills with analytic/pedagogic skills.

ii) Centralised Support

Section 2(b) of the 1981 Act uses the phrase 'educational facilities' of a kind generally provided in schools..' and presumably this encompasses the elements of service delivery reviewed in the previous sections. It could be said - tongue

firmly in cheek - that an LEA which does not provide that
range of skills and attitudes will 'statement' more pupils to
compensate for the consequently higher levels of unmet need.
In reality the same LEAs for the same budgetary reasons will
not want to have resources committed by the statutory
requirements of a statement. Nevertheless, whatever
arguments there are about the balance between 'general' and
'centralised' provision some elements of every LEAs service
delivery will continue to fall into the latter category.
This does not have to be a literal administrative or
geographic centralisation; it can be the direction of a
service from outside the mainstream aimed at children located
across that structure.

The relatively small number of children involved are
those who would suffer a greater degree of educational
handicap without the specialist teaching provided from these
centralised resources. Whether that educational handicap is
described as a learning or a teaching difficulty has more
than semantic significance - it will serve to define the
boundaries of the centralised service and the children it
envelops. The latter will not necessarily have 'severe or
complex' disabilities, some relatively minor and temporary
problems could justify this response. Agreement about the
service will probably be greatest in relation to pupils with
bio-physical or sensory problems affecting sight, hearing,
communication or movement. The implicit, rather than
statutory, categorisation of pupils with minor disabilities,
'learning difficulties' or emotional-behavioural problems is
more contentious and beyond the scope of this paper.

Some LEAs will be criticised for encompassing all these
groups within a centralised service and thereby creating an
unnecessary distinction between the identified pupils and
their peers. Others will reduce the centralised service to a
minimum and then be accused of underestimating need in their
area. The kind of perspectives which inform LEA decisions -
philosophical, financial or whatever - will hardly be swayed
from HMI reports or DES guidelines on the proportion of
teachers who should hold a specialist qualification. Nor is
there anything in Warnock or The Act which commits LEAs to
any particular kind(s) of model. Financial constraints,
professional interests and consumer lobbies will provide the
main rationale for decision-making and there are bound to be
wide regional variations reflecting what Neville Jones calls
'policy incrementalism' (1983). In the typical style of
English educational-policy change the keynotes will be
compromise with the existing framework and piecemeal
responses to adjustments elsewhere in the system.

The elementary examination of special provision

described in Jones's paper or undertaken by ILEAs committee of enquiry under the chairmanship of John Fish is much rarer than the warp and weft approach to the management of educational innovation. The latter, confined to historial frames and limited new thread, allows little scope for radical patterns. The historial framework around the periphery of mainstream schools has been largely based on the provision of places in special schools or units with a small number of pupils sustained by peripatetic teachers. But thread provided by Warnock and the 1981 Act is already looking worn; note has been made of the neglect of the Report's priority areas, consumer rights remain a contentiously ambiguous area and the abolished categories show every sign of making a come-back through the new revised (1984) version of Form 7M. It is generally expected that there will be some recomposition of centralised services with a reduction in special school placements and an increase in the use of units and peripatetic services. The worrying thing is where that process will stop and what its contours will be if it is quarried by incidental politics.

Meanwhile teacher education cannot adopt a neutral position - *pace* its own vulnerability to incidental politicians - and should produce staff who not only grasp the pedagogic requirements and specialist skills but can also facilitate their establishment in the wide context of schooling. Teachers have not previously had a formal introduction to these demands - over 70 per cent of teachers in special schools have no additional specialist qualification specifically related to special educational needs and many of those who do are in posts where the qualification is mandatory. It will therefore be a vast experience both in numbers and in the breadth of content to train personnel for the centralised services. Moreover these teachers will need a longer opportunity for study and practice than the one term '3/83' type courses allow. The idea has already been floated that the professional development required justifies the claim that this should be called 'post-experience initial training'. Given a previously sound teaching background with sufficient mainstream experience teachers in this field will need a one year or equivalent course leading to a recognised qualification.

These courses would have to offer specialist insight into the problems and solutions of teaching for particular kinds of special educational need: teaching with limited access to visual sources; teaching pupils with physical disabilities; pre-school provision; organisation for the 16 to 19 age group; or whatever other examples arise. Given the present unsettled state of the special education service and the obstinant refusal of pupils to correspond neatly to discrete categories, institutions and courses which offer a variety of options with potential cross-referencing should be more attractive to the education service and to individual students. They offer a welcome degree of flexibility, the former in the development of a career, however modest or ambitious.

Participants on one-year courses should also have the opportunity to examine and evaluate the interaction between child, family, school and community which actually creates and defines special need. They should understand the potential for change in any one of those components as the means of reducing handicap or meeting need and be developing practical strategies for encouraging that breadth of change.

Finally, this group of specialists may develop an important role in the in-service education of their colleagues through local advisory services or through contributions to higher education courses. Even if this is not the case their basic work requires a great sensitivity to communication and motivation. It would be wrong to presume that teachers who have had those skills in abundance in the classroom will naturally translate them into work with adults. This is another area with which the one-year courses will have to be concerned.

Given a broad basis which contextualises their specialist skills teachers who have followed a long course should be able to put the experience to profitable use in the full range of provision, ordinary schools, special schools, units of various kinds or peripatic work.

Servicing the Service

Two final, brief points have to be made about the servicing of the service delivery model.

The first is that teachers are not the only people who are concerned with or about the education of the children with special needs. Some of the others have a 'professional' role (notably in education management, the Health Service or Social Services) some do not (notably parents and ancillary staff). Irrespective of their ascribed status - which is rarely a true reflection of their importance or value to the children - there should be some way for each of these groups to develop their own knowledge and insight into children's educational needs. Perhaps more importantly in the parochial field of teacher development there should be some way for teachers to hear and learn from the insights and preoccupations of other groups. This multiple input of valid experiences has great potential whilst any other approach makes two unnecessary and unjustifiable presumptions, one about the value of alternative perspectives, the other about the need for teachers to make informed judgements.

The second point to be made about servicing the delivery model is the difficulty higher education establishments are going to have adapting themselves to provide for the teacher education requirements which have been outlined. If the general awareness about special needs is to permeate teaching courses, then the institutions will have to develop integrated, coherent plans for its inclusion.

Even presuming a transfer of resources from initial into in-service courses the burden of providing this element cannot fall on the existing specialists. It is not just too big a task, it is that such an approach would still contradict the general, widespread responsibilities identified in the first part of this paper. It would be a remarkable irony if the institutions tried to promote that idea of 'every teacher a special needs teacher' without their own staff adopting the principle in their own work.

Where there are 'special needs specialists' already in the colleges their role will have to be re-assessed much as the role of 'special needs specialists' in the school system has been. Colleges will also have to look at their place in the network which is responding to special needs and, recognising that it no longer consists of discrete inaccessible elements, ask how they can use as well as support the other elements. This is a longer term process in which the links between practitioners and colleges - already signalled in the White Paper on Teaching Quality - will play a critical part.

Summary and Conclusion

The Warnock Report and the 1981 Education Act have created an atmosphere of change within the field of special education but are ill-equipped to fulfil the expectations they have created. Such change as may take place will be as a result of the endogenous connections between special and mainstream provision and will reflect a much wider range of pressures than those generally acknowledged to concern Warnock and the Act. The function of teacher training is not just to prepare teachers for new roles - which are partly unpredictable - but also to prepare them to be catalysts in the creation of new roles.

The fundamental principles of comprehensive schooling

challenge the notion that special educational needs consistently require expertise from specialists or from institutions whose boundaries are well defined. Instead the service delivery model should adopt notional or actual networks of personnel and provision. Specialist support will be available but this should increasingly dovetail with mainstream classroom practice and reflect aspects of learning theories which apply to all children. There will need to be corresponding provision for teaching training: in all courses for 'classroom' teachers; in one term or equivalent courses for designated teachers with wider responsibilities in one, or at the most a very few schools; and in one year courses for specialist teachers and advisory personnel who will staff an LEA's centralised services.

Chapter Four

A WHOLE-SCHOOL APPROACH TO MEETING ALL NEEDS

John Sayer

At the start of this volume, we showed how ACSET has tried recently to plan a full programme of training for diversity, meeting the needs of teachers in different local situations, many of them changing rapidly. We suggested that one of the likely future contexts is a whole-school and community education model; and that this poses particular problems for training with a focus on special educational needs. Later chapters offer different solutions; this one seeks only to describe more fully what can be offered by enlisting the whole resource of a neighbourhood's education service, and to illustrate some of the issues for training.

Most teachers would want to be able to help respond to the needs of all children. The separation of special education and of special services from the mainstream of schools and colleges is now seen to have been the result of outmoded and discredited attitudes towards handicap and the handicapped; but re-integration of children with special education needs to the continuum of a whole community, in and out of schools, presents serious problems. Where do we start with a fourteen-year-old boy who has been recommended on removal to transfer after seven years in special schools; and whose voluminous file from schools, local authority, and educational psychologists contains not one mention of what has been learnt, what have been his interests, or what curricular programme might be recommended for the future? That happens to be on my desk while writing; it has engaged a group of senior colleagues in a whirl of activity in the last week; and next week, there will be a challenge to a dozen teachers and scores of pupils to reach out and accommodate an unknown quantity, himself being subjected to an unknown world. It ought not to look like that; perhaps in future years it will not; but right now, it does, and we are not fully prepared for the change.

We scream for support, from 'those who know', but nobody knows what will happen in this different context. There are no other experts. Educational psychologists have not yet come to terms with the upper secondary school curriculum for which their advice is sought. Special school teachers have no idea how this boy will fare in large groups. There is the negative reassurance that all has not been well in recent years, and that a change might not be a bad thing. Such is the sum total of a ream of slavish testing and assessment through the separate system. Now this is an exceptional case; but special education has been built around exceptions. It would be very easy to build a model of integration in much the same way, with special units on site, specialist staff responsible for children placed in the unit, and support staff to advise ordinary teachers what they can and cannot do to help.

The Warnock Committee came up with the same contradictory solutions which are to be found in this volume; the contradictions are to be expected in a period of transition; but they are now standing in the way of transition. Do we extend special education to provide a resource for integration wherever possible, or do we extend what we have supposed to be the mainstream, to provide a resource planned to meet all needs? The rubric of the 1981 Act enshrines the rhetoric of mainstreaming; but the regulations guarantee separation in attitudes, resources, records, and responses.

Because of these confusions, and because of existing structures and habits, many local authorities have fallen into the trap of believing they are responding to cries for help among 'ordinary' schoolteachers, by strengthening the special services under the banner of 'support' to the ordinary school. Appointments are made to peripatetic 'teams', or to off-site 'centres'. These support and strengthen each other by creating 'support groups' or steering groups, and acquire separate resource-bases and support staff. The support teacher assigned to a particular school is drawn back into a protective, sympathetic network of fellow-sufferers. One local authority has been discovered to have no fewer than 360 such appointments; and the effect on children is unknown. Once the interest-group of fellow-professionals is turned in upon itself, ordinary teachers, already de-skilled and patronised by the concept and practice of 'support', are made to believe that they have no resource, cannot cope alone, and must look to support services to take on problems themselves. So the circle is completed, back to special education. Separate management of professional groups leads eventually to separate management of children.

The main thrust of development towards an integrated service to children should be under the aegis of mainstream schools and colleges, rather than through separate administrative channels. If above we have written of 'enlisting the whole resource of a neighbourhood's education service', there is a task not just of attitudinal change, but of management. Schools and colleges exist in a professional and administrative context as well as a physical proximity to the people they serve; there is no long-term future in school reforms which run counter to LEA practice. So this chapter supposes, in outlining a way of life for schools, that parallel transformations are occurring in local administration, and in specialised services. If all teachers are to feel a responsibility to all children, then all officers and advisors should have their brief extended too. Educational psychologists, school social workers, multicultural 'teams', careers officers, peripatetic music teachers, should work to school groups. The funding of separate services, at present tied to different sections with discrete budgets sometimes under separate sub-committees, should be identified, secured according to new criteria, and channelled through the ordinary school services. The Special Education Section of LEA administration should be amalgamated with the office equivalent of the mainstream. If we are pointing towards a multi-professional service to local communities, a start could be made by fusing educational and social services in the local authority, instead of interpreting corporate management as throwing inadequate meat to a hungry pack of wolves in the same cage at a zoo.

This organisational problem is by no means confined to special education, and it would be wrong to try to solve it as though it were. Indeed, the less the focus on special educational needs as now defined, the better will be the chances of growing into a more complete coverage of all educational needs in a locality. A resource approach to meeting special needs is only likely to be successful as part and parcel of an overall management of resources for all local educational services. We have to ask what that looks like in a school; but in doing so, we also have to ask what a school will look like as part of a corporately managed local resource.

This means that even some of the bold innovations already made in the cause of integration may have to be confined to the shorter term. Where, for example, we have established a bridge across primary and secondary schooling, in recognition of the particular importance of continuity in responding to special educational needs, the bridge may have to be broadened

57

to take the whole school population across that great divide. Instead of accepting that at the age of eleven all children change suddenly from a whole-curricular and generalist-teacher context to one in which the curriculum and the school day are cut to pieces, bringing intolerable problems to children with special needs, we may wish to extend more defined areas of curriculum from a gradual introduction at an earlier age towards a less rigidly subject-bound approach through to the age of fourteen or so. If that happens for all children - and there are strong indications that even the DES is pointing that way - then the case for a distinct primary-secondary linkage for special educational needs only will be less strong.

The issues which at present centre on strategies of withdrawal from ordinary classes or of co-operative resourcing within them are largely determined by the current assumptions that in secondary schools at any rate the school day is organised in groups of thirty. That could also change, and probably should. Once it is accepted that children should learn and continue to work in small groups of no more than five or six, with the teacher as the organiser of learning experiences rather than out in front talking four-fifths of the time to a whole non-group of thirty, there is a shift in the whole language of resourcing, and coping in 'the ordinary classroom'.

Most attention has been given to coping skills and support in the ordinary classroom as though this were the whole of school education. Although the intention is to enable children with special educational needs to take part in as full a range as possible of a school's activity, support services are organised to assist in the formal curriculum only. Once schools begin to organise themselves according to the whole of their planned contribution to learning, and include what has been curiously described as extra-curricular in their fabric of organisation, the nature of the school day is bound to change, and a variety of modular approaches to this new admixture of formal and non-formal school education will emerge. It is likely that many of those services which have been organised as interruptions to the normal routine - music instrument teaching, personal counselling, field study trips, work experience, remedial attention, tutorial discussion - will be brought into a much more flexible framework extending beyond the present notional nine to four timetable in the school term. As soon as an organisation recognises and extends to all the activities generated by a school, there is a commitment to offering all these learning opportunities to everyone in the system, and adjusting resources of all kinds accordingly.

Yet another change may be expected in home-school co-operation. Schools are developing into community centres for learning, bringing together learners of all ages whom they have previously kept apart, and bringing courses of a less formal kind for adults and young people into the same programme of opportunities. Home-school links will not only be stronger as a result, but of a different working order. Special educators have previously put more emphasis on working with parents than have many in the mainstream; and it has been accepted more readily that these links are necessary as a support to children with special educational needs. However, many ordinary schools have developed this part of their work already, and many more are likely to do so over the next few years. The nature of linkage could well change too. The traditional parent-teacher association may survive, with its minority of energetic committed parents seeking in vain to involve the majority. Parental involvement in governing bodies will also increase, with a cumbersome machinery of election. These are no more than the formal recognition of what should and could be happening at a personal level.

The form tutor in a secondary school is emerging as the focus for a radical shift in organisation. Coherence in the curriculum requires the tutor as the agent, relating different courses to the overall needs of a pupil, and of the small learning groups of pupils which have been envisaged. Already, it has been established that parents can relate more readily to the form tutor than to the whole of the school organisation at one go; and that discussion in depth with one tutor is more likely to bring parents and teachers together than the mass meetings which make such demands on those parents who can be free on one occasion. What is now being explored is whether parents in small groups, if possible the groups which have been formed for pupils, can contribute more fully and more easily than through the top-down PTAs and governing bodies as we know them. An organisation developed from parent-teacher-pupil cells has meaning for everyone. This is bound to come as schools identify the context of learning experience of which they are only a part, but to which they can bring a skilled resource and focus. If that happens, pupils will be able to benefit from the rapid growth of information and potentially educative experience available at home and elsewhere.

Schools and the Future

The whole notion of 'going to school' to 'get an education' derives from a past in which there was no other means of acquiring knowledge or of transmitting it to large numbers. Nowadays, schools are by no means the only source of education. Radio, telephones, travel, television and now videos and the micro-computer have become accessible to most, and will be used for more and more purposes. Schools contribute to a whole curriculum; the school curriculum by itself cannot be considered whole; to have sense and validity, schools must work in context, the context of the learning experience at home, through media, and in the local community. To do that, schools have to be seen as a community resource, contributing, sharing, using and being used by any who are engaged in learning or helping to learn.

Distinctions of age have to be blurred; knowledge and needs are changing so fast that nobody can be said to have completed an initial education. If the school becomes a family and neighbourhood resource rather than just an institution in which to place children of a particular age, then it is also more likely to be accessible to those with special educational needs, and to respond flexibly. That is just one part of the coverage of a school for the whole local community, which identifies what it can best contribute to local education in the round.

Of course, once we go down that road, the notion of a school curriculum as such becomes as untenable as the idea of a balanced diet in school meals without regard to what is being eaten between times. There will still be concerns for a broad, balanced and relevant curriculum which includes or is completed by schools; but to discover that, schools, parents and others in the locality have to work together and plan together with young learners. That demands a different kind of teacher, a different set of relationships, and a different kind of training.

It probably requires a different kind of school too. Schools ought to become multi-professional, starting with the integration of specific professional services within the education business. Educational social workers, counsellors, careers officers, educational psychologists, peripatetic remedial and multicultural services, ought to be part of the same show. Alternative education, now too often expressed in off-site sanctuaries, shelters, or sin-bins, should be part of the same mainstream service, recognised and supported from within. To work that way, not only teachers but the specific professionals have to learn to work together, not by referral and chain-reaction, but in concert under the same management.

That again is a matter of preparation and should affect the nature of teacher-training.

Nowhere more than in providing for children with special educational needs is it apparent that a school framework based on year-groups and age-bands is inappropriate. A continuum of response across age-sectors is more important a notion than a continuum of response across the bands of general to specific, or integration to segregation. That may mean facing the fact that current divisions between primary, secondary and further education, or between these and various forms of youth and community or adult and continuing education, are artificial, limiting, and unnecessary for more than specified purposes. In Denmark, it would seem curious to describe as comprehensive a school which did not span primary and secondary ages, or a local service which did not provide fully for adult education. So we may have to move away from the current government insistence on training teachers for specific ages, and look towards a local federation of education services and the ability of teachers to stretch the system and themselves.

Equally essential is a wider range of teaching styles and skills than at present envisaged in initial training criteria. There are encouraging signs of a rebirth of team approaches to teaching, and the new frameworks for courses in upper secondary education demand concerted attention by teams to a range of skills not necessarily identified with subject specialisms. CGLI, TVEI and CPVE approaches are on the increase. This more general adoption of co-operative modes of teaching should help the partnership between 'special' and 'specialist' teachers working together to change, extend and bring about the normal work of ordinary groups including those with identified special learning needs. They ought not to be the only ones sharing and team-teaching; it is because they are unusual in being more than one to a class that they are seen to be unnecessarily special. So again, teaching in partnership has to be a part of training and staff development.

Because of this much wider function of schools and teachers, and because of the spread of specific professional skills across a team of teachers and others, certain professional disciplines will be recognised as essential for all and not the prerogative of a distinct group. The whole field of identification of need and of assessment is one which will be shared, and training will have to do with that sharing. It will tend to focus on learning needs for shorter and more specific purposes; and assessment of performance will be subsumed in assessment of needs for further learning rather than on certification as a passport without expiry date.

61

A contextual approach to meeting all local needs and organising resources to do so points, therefore, to a shift in emphasis for the training of teachers, all teachers. This appears to have been recognised in current adjustments to initial training and in proposals for the specialised training which may follow. Even more important, however, will be the in-service self-development of everyone together in localities, with a focus on the pooling of skills, on contributions to the whole curriculum not only in school but in the home and community, on personal tutoring not as a separate pastoral function but as the key relationship in making the best possible sense of all educational experiences of individuals in groups, and on skills of assessment identifying positive achievement and indicating future life-chances.

Chapter Five

TRAINING FOR TEAMWORK

Patricia Potts

Those concerned with meeting the needs of children who face difficulties in school are constantly encouraged to work more closely together. Why should teachers, nurses, social workers, psychologists, doctors, work together? What is the purpose of inter-professional teamwork and where does the idea come from? Evaluating the rhetoric has to precede any discussion of an appropriate training syllabus.

Inter-professional Cooperation

A series of official documents published between 1972 and 1983 call repeatedly for cooperation between statutory authorities, specifically in relation to children under five and children with 'special educational needs'. The 1972 White Paper 'Education: a Framework for Expansion' advocated cooperation in making provision for under-fives and the Joint Consultative Committees, set up after the reorganisation of the National Health Service in 1973, represent the formal machinery through which the health, education and social services can work together. The Departments of Health and Social Security and Education and Science sent out a letter in March 1976 on 'Coordination of Local Authority Services for Children Under Five' which included the following reasons for cooperation. First, as the early years are so vital to a child's development and therefore to subsequent problems, all resources should be used to maximum advantage. Second, because provisions are inadequate and new resources are not forthcoming, the only way to improve the situation is by increasing the effectiveness of what already exists. The letter argued that 'a knowledge of the juxtaposition of services is often as valuable as the integration of services'.

A similar letter sent out in January 1978, headed

'Coordination of Services for Children Under Five' added these reasons for inter-authority cooperation: first, that cooperation was essential for full and accurate assessment of the needs of under-fives; second, that cooperation was sensible when making referrals to pre-school provisions because of the range of organisations involved in running them; and third, that liaison should be automatic between those involved in home-visiting schemes so that families are not bewilderingly flooded by professional attention.

The Warnock Report, also 1978, advocates cooperation between statutory authorities in two contexts: first, in connection with recommendations for professional training; and second, in connection with plans for providing advice to the education authorities on what health and social services should be provided for pupils with special needs in ordinary schools. The 1981 Education Act refers to collaboration between the statutory authorities in Schedule 1, Part 1: Assessments, Regulations (2): 'medical, psychological and educational advice as may be prescribed' is to be collected in the process of assessing the special educational needs of children. Circular 1/83 'Assessments and Statements of Special Educational Needs', gives details of this collaboration; gathering together a range of opinions enables professionals 'to arrive at a more complete understanding of a child's special educational needs', but 'the ultimate responsibility for assessing the child's special educational needs rests with the LEA':

> In many instances, it will be sufficient for professional advisers to submit their advice separately to the LEA. It may be desirable for professional assessment to proceed in sequence, educational advice being followed by medical advice and then by psychological advice. (para 32).
>
> Effective multi-professional work is not easy to achieve. It requires cooperation, collaboration and mutual support. Each professional adviser needs to be aware of the rôles of his colleagues and should seek to reach agreement with them on their several rôles and functions. It follows from this that his advice should reflect his own concerns, leaving others to concentrate on their particular area of expertise.
>
> (DES, 1983, para. 3)

These views of professional cooperation do not require live discussion or shared decision-making. They do not imply any merging or swapping of tasks. Cooperation is seen as a way

64

of making assessment procedures and the use of existing
facilities more efficient and effective and it is defined in
terms which promote mutual respect for separate areas of
expertise. Teamwork is doing your own thing unchallenged, but
letting the others know. Reverence for specialisation means
that the official version, despite being presented as the way
to overcome the isolation of professionals, does not imply any
significant changes in, nor any critical examination of,
current working practices.

Training and Teamwork

Should we be surprised or not, therefore, that the report
of the Advisory Committee on the Supply and Education of
Teachers (ACSET) on 'Teacher Training and Special Educational
Needs (1984) contains no description of inter-professional
teamwork or an outline of training approaches? The document
focuses on individual teacher-quality and career prospects.
Changing all teachers' attitudes and increasing their
responsibility for teaching pupils who face difficulties in
school are major themes of the report, but they are not set in
the context of a developing educational system. Indeed, the
government's remit to the Committee in 1983 somehow forgot
about the Warnock report and only referred to children in
special schools and units, that is, a range of segregated and
semi-segregated provisions. The Committee decided at once to
expand on this narrow brief:

> 'It is ... clearly vital that all teachers should be
> alert to the existence of children with special
> educational needs... We have thought it important
> that our recommendations should related both to the
> training of teachers taking specific responsibility
> for pupils with special educational needs, whether in
> special or in ordinary schools, and more generally,
> to the training needs of all teachers in this
> respect' (ACSET, 1984, para. 1)

However, it is assumed that the pattern of mainstream and
separated special schools will continue, that the extent of
integration will depend upon resources within LEAs and that
there will always be children who 'cannot' be included in
ordinary schools:

> There is no indication that a point might be reached
> where an LEA sees no need to maintain separate
> special provision: rather, it seems to us that the
> pupil population of such establishments will consist
> increasingly of the profoundly and/or multiply
> handicapped, and of children with severe emotional,
> behavioural and learning problems, requiring support

> which cannot be provided in ordinary schools, or a
> curriculum specifically designed to meet their
> particular learning difficulties.

(ACSET, 1984, para. 3)

So the institutional bases for proposed changes in attitudes
and practices are envisaged as remaining unchanged, as if they
are outside the range of factors which make these changes easy,
difficult or impossible.

It is true that the report does expect an increase in
mixed ability groupings in ordinary schools:

> We are convinced that all initial teacher training
> courses must prepare their students to meet the needs
> of the full range of pupils in ordinary schools.
> This range encompasses a significant number of
> children who from time to time will have special
> educational needs; but will not experience a change
> of school setting, and responsibility for meeting
> those needs is not an option, but an integral part of
> the job.

(ACSET, 1984, para. 6)

To this extent, therefore, the ACSET document supports a
generic approach to initial teacher training. Paragraph 14 of
the report describes how specialised initial training courses
for teachers of children with severe learning difficulties did
attract a high standard of student and, during the 1970s, were
necessary to fill the jobs created by the new 'ESN(S)' schools
following the reception of those children into the education
system. However, jobs are now vacant on the same scale in a
new sort of school and 'It would, in our view, be quite
inappropriate for courses of initial training, leading to
qualified teacher status, to concentrate on producing teachers
for this highly specialist and very limited field of
employment' (ACSET, 1984, para. 14, ii). Specialisation is not
rejected, however, only delayed for in-service courses later
on. The scheme of in-service training described in paragraph
10 of the ACSET report does recognise that teachers may want to
change specialisms, that 'the kinds of specialisation needed
are likely to be developing and changing rapidly over the next
few years' but the aim of this in-service training is to
provide LEAs with 'expert advice' from their 'detailed
knowledge of the spectrum of special educational needs and the
responses required' (para. 10, iii). This kind of training
leaves no room for asking inclusive questions about children
within an educational setting and, by reserving the discussion

of a particular group of children for a particular group of teachers, it segregates both pupils and freshly-trained teachers.

The ACSET report outlines changes in the approach to training and teaching for those to work with children who have special educational needs but against a very sketchy background of a similarly changing system. There is a concern that all teachers should be willing and prepared to meet special needs where they occur in ordinary schools, but no consequent concern that the ordinary school is the place where special needs should be met. Thus the ACSET-trained specialist fits into the world of collaborating experts described in the documents I have quoted rather than into a world of cooperative-teaching or mixed ability groupings.

Teamwork in Practice

The exemplar of the professional team, of course, is that of the hospital consultant and dependent group of practitioners. Such a team is hierarchical in structure, is not multi-professional and does work together on a daily basis. This sort of team therefore differs considerably from distantly collaborating multi-professional groups assessing the special educational needs of children. Would you call their postal advice-sharings either 'teamwork' or 'cooperation'? If not, what would genuinely multi- professional practices look like? How far would they be possible? What sort of changes would be entailed? Can people be trained to work together? Is 'teamwork' different from 'working cooperatively'?

Between 1974 and 1978 I worked as the teacher in a multi-professional child guidance clinic team, about ten people (social workers, psychiatrists, teacher, psychotherapist, psychologists) with very different status, pay, training backgrounds and styles of working. The medical model of teamwmork was just beginning to be eroded and replaced by a two-tiered system of management with a triumvirate of senior social worker, consultant psychiatrist and educational psychologist taking major decisions and responsibility. It proved to be difficult for the psychiatrist to give up the boss's role, however, particularly because of expectations from outside, from the LEA, from the hospital where several team members worked, from local referring agencies. The extent of practical teamwork varied: working together in pairs with families was a regular occurrence and partnerships flourished from time to time. Using the twice weekly team meetings to develop a plan of work was also common. Much of what was designed to be the therapeutic work of the clinic was influenced by active teamwork. With assessment it was different.   Assessments of the psychological, social or educational needs of the children were often remotely controlled affairs, with one-to-one interviews and reports going through the pigeon-holes for compilation, as if assessment was the real test of a professional's right to the title and had to be safeguarded by an uncontaminated privacy, justified by the bearing of individual responsibility.   It could be argued that shortage of time keeps professionals apart but this shortage of time is built in to a clinic team in which traditionally the most prestigious members are part-time, adding to their scarcity value and dividing up their professional commitment.   If this sort of team is supportive of families or of its members then it is in spite of, rather than because of its structure.

The notion of effective teamwork has a familiar set of implications: efficiency, speed, successful resolution of crises, continuity, strength, back-up support and a greater wealth of resources than the same number of people working on their own.   The notion of cooperative work has a different set, including respect both for what it feels like to be a member of a professional team and for what it feels like to be one of the team's clients.   Cooperative work implies a sharing of tasks, responsibility, conditions of employment, control of resources. Teamwork, therefore, can be more or less, or not at all, cooperative.

Devising and writing an Open University course, editing collections of case studies and articles, making audio and video tapes - all these require teamwork which, when it goes well and is enjoyable, becomes cooperative.   The most successful kinds of teamwork I have experienced have been in connection with organising seminars and conferences with people from a range of institutional bases and in connection with parents groups who are seeking to change educational policy-making in their local areas.   The teamwork was lubricated by the shared commitment, which guaranteed a high level of energy and concentration, by the explicit aim of the joint venture, by the sharing of tasks, by the fairly small numbers of people involved and by the irrelevance of status hierarchies within the groups.   While it is true that a variety of experience is useful, it is the minimising of differences which characterises teamwork.   This seems to be lacking in many multi-professional teams now at large.

Sally Tomlinson (1982) shows that inter-professional collaboration in the assessment of the educational needs of children is marked by competition rather than by cooperation. The accounts given by headteachers, doctors and psychologists of children placed within a single educational category (formerly 'educationally subnormal', now euphemised as 'having moderate learning difficulties') reveal as many different professional languages. Sally Tomlinson concludes that:

> The development of extended "multi-professional" assessment, advocated by both the court and the Warnock reports ... assumes an unrealistic degree of communication, cooperation, and absence of professional conflicts and jealousies.
>
> Tomlinson, 1982, p.31)

When did you last work as part of a team? What sort of project was involved? Was the teamwork cooperative? If not, would a course of training have made it so? Was the teamwork in fact anything to do with your professional working life? It seems to be that mixed groups of professionals work together as a team when they like each other, when their conditions of service are equalised or when they work from a despecialised base like a combined nursery centre or a community college. Is not multi-professional teamwork almost a contradition in terms? Does not a 'team' cease to be 'multi-professional', regardless of whether it is hierarchical or cooperative?

Teamwork and Specialisation

I have argued that it is shared commitment, both to a style of working and to a view of a system that is worth working towards, that makes for teamwork between professionals and that, by implication, most training courses encourage separateness and rivalry. This does not mean that there are no implications for the revision of training courses, however. Quite the reverse. But in designing courses that would promote teamwork between practising professionals we have to examine the pressures which at the moment tend to keep them apart. What do existing courses include and exclude? What do professional team members need to know, and who decides? Should potential team members train together? Where should they train?

The following areas might be relevant to a training course that provided the opportunity for students both to develop a critical awareness of the system in which they were going to work and to work out an initial view of the system in which they would like to work:

1. Discussion of their own possibile roles, the writings and teachings which are their sources, and the context of their development.

2. Who are their potential clients? Why? What are their perspectives and changing experiences?

3. What is the range of existing provisions, services, other personnel?

4. How has this framework been influenced by social, economic, legal, political factors?

5. How do historical, comparative, future perspectives help to account for the present system?

It should be possible for students to use their own, varying, questions to re-structure courses and to participate in the arrangements for practical work.

But generic courses which include students who will eventually work under different professional names, like large-scale versions of the modular courses now developing for initial teacher trainees, are in decline, actually discouraging respect for the integration of professional worlds. What is it about specialists that attracts and what is it about generic workers that repels? Specialists have high standards of skill and knowledge, they are experts, they have a clearly-defined responsibility for their work, they have prestigious careers and good salaries, they provide a tailor-made service. How far is all this either true or desirable? Generic workers, in contrast, have no specific purpose, being all-purpose; they are consequently uncertain about their role and responsibility and they have a low status and low salaries. How far is this true? It could be argued, alternatively, that specialists become inflexible, that they lead unnecessarily secret lives, that they perpetuate divisions between client groups and between other professionals. Generic workers, on the other hand, belong to communities rather than to institutions; they can be flexible, they can share responsibility with colleagues and clients and they do not perpetuate stigmatising categorisation.

In 'The Professionals' (1982), Unit 7 of our Open University course 'Special Needs in Education' (E241), I discussed the generic-specialist debate and pointed out that a broad professional training was advocated in the 1950s, although it was with the view of making the career of a psychologist more attractive:

> A training course...for work in either the educational or the health services would widen the field of opportunity and so make the career of a psychologist far more attractive...The difference in the work of the two services need be no obstacle to

the provision of a common training ... Towards the
end of courses a certain amount of specialisation,
mainly in the practical work undertaken, could be
introduced.

(Ministry of Education, 1955)

A similar pattern was introduced for social workers by the
Seebohm Report (1968). The generic training course is:

... a broad introduction to the knowledge required
by a social case worker, and is designed to be taken
by students whose subsequent job experience will
vary considerably. It simplifies the organization of
training for a hybrid profession and is potentially
flexible, preparing workers for changing rôles. The
Certificate in Social Work is planned by CCETSW to
be a generic course for those who will later work
with groups of handicapped children and adults. In
1959, the Younghusband Report on local authority
social workers envisaged a course for health
visitors, social workers, occupational therapists
and residential care staff (para. 889).

One educational psychologist "sees no reason why you cannot
have a generic kind of psychologist...Many of the skills
involved in dealing with people at different age levels and
stages of development are similar" (Loxley, 1978).

Any professional whose clients (though perhaps nominally a
homogeneous group) present a wide range of problems will
perform an essentially generic rôle, despite years of
specialist training. Critics of the generic approach argue that
it leads to superficial, naive practice. In his introduction to
a series of transcribed interviews with the parents of
handicapped children, Dr Mervyn Fox writes;

There is no doubt that many of these families
present extreme technical problems for the generic
social workers, who is faced with demands for
practical development advice, information on
environmental resources of a highly specialized
nature, and interpretation of the actions of the
half-dozen other professionals involved as well as
the need for utilizing knowledge of the unconscious
implications of overt behaviour and general
emotional factors...my personal prescription is
unavowedly one of a return to specialization....
This is not to decry the value of a generic
training, but only to emphasize what I see as the
impossibility of generic practice (Fox, 1975).

One psychologist I know said: "In order to become reasonably proficient in any sphere you have to specialize. A counsellor, psychotherapist or social worker can give support to the family. I'd find that very difficult". But there's no reason why a professional should work in isolation; in their book on the education of slow learning and maladjusted children, Galloway and Goodwin suggest that "there is a world of difference between a generic social worker and a generic *team* containing specialists in different fields" (1979).

Changing the structure of professional training to encourage inter-professional teamwork is a process which therefore has to reckon with increasingly strong pressures towards specialisation and competitive standards and the extent of the changes that would be necessary throws the present system into an identity crisis. An example of just how feverish is the temperature of resistance to a more comprehensive system of provision and training is the series of articles and letters published in the 'Times Educational Supplement' during September and October, 1983.

The Effects of Training

So what is the rôle of training within the education and welfare systems? Does the content of training courses confirm trends that are already taking place or trends that local authorities and central government want to confirm? Can people be trained to do something new, or to change their practice later? Mrs. Warnock has outlined her own ideas for a lengthy process of undergraduate and graduate, academic and practical work leading to a fully-fledged specialist special educator:

> The "skills, understanding and appreciation" that "must be developed if the aims of the special education element" (to be included in all initial training courses) are to be realized are the following: "awareness of the range of career and professional opportunities in special education, the availability of further qualifications in special education, and the fact that special education offers the teachers engaged in it an intellectual challenge of the highest order".

(DES, 1978, paras. 12.7/8)

Mary Warnock is sensitive to the low status that has been the professional lot of those working in special schools, but the trouble with her plan is that it would perpetuate the separate identity of the 'special' as opposed to the ordinary teacher and runs the risk of training being carried on in comparative isolation from changing provisions. And here we have another contradiction: including a 'special education element' in all initial training courses, but using it to transmit a separatist message. Professional evolution in terms of blurring the edges of traditional rôles in response to a developing education system and the changing perceptions of what children need within it would be precluded by this fundamentally specialist approach, which contains no exploration of the features of the most comprehensive schools, such as cooperative and team teaching or small, stable, mixed-ability groupings, which could facilitate the fusion of special and mainstream education.

Another version of the specialist special educator was described by Peter Mittler in 'Special Education-Forward Trends' (June 1981). Again, there is little attempt to look at a special education in the context of the system as a whole and no critique of the rôle special schools play:

> 'The last ten years have seen an astonishing development of knowledge and skills in special education. Although there are still major gaps in our knowledge, the speed and scale of *progress* are such that all of us must consider ourselves unqualified and out of date in relation to the demands of tomorrow'.(my italics)

Mittler believes that this represents a move away from a clinical style of professional work towards a social one, keeping the child in his or her home environment. But the kind of work to be undertaken by the professionals still consists of assessment and intensive, exhaustive schemes of exercises which treat the child in isolation, although at home; and it seems to me to be very much like old-style clinical sessions, a kind of compensatory treatment. Mittler's style of working with families is quite compatible with the views of those who argue that children under five belong at home with their mothers. Specialisation may work to reduce the options open to the consumers of services.

Mittler gives a paralysing list of skills for the teacher to develop, based on 'proficiency in the specification of behavioural objectives, goal setting, task analysis, programme writing, a range of prompting, shaping, chaining and reinforcement techniques and generalisation training'. All of which makes the education of young children with special needs very complicated, technical abstract, individualistic, artificial. And, whereas repeated practice may help a child to perform a task, there is a danger that the professional will also treat the parents like pupils. The Portage scheme which is now popular with pre-school peripatetic teachers covers every aspect of behaviour you can think of, which does not leave parents much room to do things their way.

Mary Warnock's vision of training resembles that of an educational psychologist. In 1938 Cyril Burt, founder of that profession in England, argued that teachers should raise themselves by index-linking their status to that of science (i.e. psychology):

> No layman would write to "The Times" telling the doctor how to treat a patient suffering from bodily disease. But few laymen would hesitate to diagnose the mental state of a criminal they have never seen, to discuss the aims and methods of educating the normal pupils, or to lay down principles for the treatment of the dull and delinquent. The teacher has never enjoyed that sacrosanct reputation of being an expert and a specialist in his own particular sphere which the doctor has always aimed for himself...Nothing, I believe, would raise the professional status of the teacher so much as an attempt on the part of the teacher himself to turn his art into a science.

(Quoted in Sutherland and Sharp, 1980, p.191)

Both views of training support the maintenance of a considerable distance between client and expert, between expert and public opinion. Specialisation fixes territorial boundaries so that neither professionals nor 'laymen' find it easy to cross. This kind of training takes a long time and creates, in advance, a distinct role-expectation for the teacher, making moves towards a sharing of responsibility for all pupils in school, that is, inter-professional cooperation, extremely difficult. It represents training-to-be-different, not training for teamwork.

If you want to establish more genuine teamwork, this has to be reflected in the structure of training: generic courses with a wide range of options; courses must be free, accessible, informal, as short as possible, as closely attached to community work bases as possible; trainees must participate in their organisation and operation. Any one course can transmit a variety of messages and a course on meeting special educational needs in ordinary schools can tell participants that a process of integration is a good thing or that it is a bad thing. There is no guarantee that courses will ask the question 'why do children have special needs?' and the content of each will include and exclude certain issues. A further problem for teamwork is that not all members of multi-disciplinary teams will be considered as equally eligible for training. There will be citizens-above-training, the natural trainers, the experts. That is why a notion of training for teamwork is constraining, preserving the expectation of trainer-trainee, teacher-pupil, professional-client differences and distances.

Beyond Training

We have seen that official rhetoric does not promote cooperative teamwork between groups of professionals and I have discussed a range of serious obstacles to the redesigning of training courses. But it may be that knowing what these are is not nearly enough, that making it possible to share power and share rewards for work done requires structural changes which are beyond the professionals' control. That cooperative work is difficult, even when that is your explicit aim, is illustrated by an evaluation of a community project in Scotland. The client-professional tensions described by Jean Barr (1983) may be relevant to the internal difficulties of some multi-professional 'teams' (Barr, 1983).

Conclusions

Multi-professional teamwork is a rhetoric, rather than a practice, and it has been defined in terms of respecting the differences between professionals rather that in terms of their common interests as equals. The sort of training which would support the official view of teamwork therefore would function to consolidate separate, ranked, areas of expertise. Teamwork minimises the differences between professionals and concentrates on a shared, explicit goal; it can be hierarchical or cooperative in its organisation. As the current pressures to specialise and remain separate and competitive are so strong, it could be said that the ACSET document is realistic in its assumption of minimal institutional change within the education system.

Cooperative teamwork does require change, though, and does offer a critique of current practices; by aiming to reduce professional differences, by aiming to integrate training and work, and by aiming to harmonise as far as possible the interests of professionals and clients. Because cooperative teamwork is non-specialised in its approach it actually increases the possibility of efficiency, of reducing the number of different individuals separately working with any one family. People who work cooperatively do it because they want to and in many cases this may run counter to the effects of their training. Insofar as training sets up a pattern of

75

expectations about a future working role, then people who have experienced a cooperative form of training may expect and want to work in this way; it will fit in with their view of themselves as a professional.

The effect of most professional training is the practice of specialised, hierarchical teams, in whose management not all members are equally involved. Accepting the virtues of specialisation also tends to perpetuate an uncritical view of the present system and an assumption that its history is as progressive as Peter Mittler believes. For the aim of working well together in order to sift and sort out children is in itself inconsistent. As it happens, however, the sort of 'cooperation' officially required is only notional. Cooperative teamwork, in contrast, would have to include the team's clients, not hold them at arms length as objects of study and professional scrutiny. Training for teamwork must remain an unlikely proposition until the trainers want to work together as a team.

Chapter Six

SPECIAL EDUCATIONAL NEEDS AND INITIAL TRAINING

David Thomas and Colin Smith

Introduction

In this paper we have not attempted to specify a detailed
curriculum for special educational needs in initial training.
Our concern has been to identify a number of key issues which
we believe should be incorporated into the discussions which
are currently taking place on special needs and training.
Among these issues we select the following as being of
considerable importance; criteria for the selection of course
content in the context of initial training, 'awareness courses'
vs. 'skill-building courses', the dangers of encapsulating SEN
training and locating training in the current climate of
changing attitudes. We would wish to emphasise the necessity
of seeing 'special needs' as an integral part of the training
process which has as a major objective the involvement of
future teachers as active agents in promoting change. Finally
we suggest that a thorough going integration of a 'special
needs' philosophy has much to offer as a basis for re-shaping
initial training itself.

A rôle for all teachers

The Report for ACSET (1984) recommends that

> "all teachers of the 2-19 age group need to know how
> to identify the special educational needs of children
> and young people, what they can do themselves to meet
> those needs and when and how to enlist specialist
> help. This has implications for all initial teacher
> training courses ....
> (and)
> Subject specialist teachers should be equipped to
> take account of special educational needs in the

> planning and development of their curriculum area
> ..."

It is generally accepted that initial training is the first of several steps towards becoming an effective practitioner. These additional steps are provided by a variety of in-service courses and professional experience, but the initial period of training can be regarded as a significant period in which certain values are incorporated which can sustain practice even when confronted with staffroom cynicism. Initial training has many tasks among which we would select

(a)   confidence and skill-building for immediate rôles (teaching practice and first appointment)
(b)   developing a number of perspectives on the teacher's rôle and the way the education system operates and
(c)   making the student aware of a range of issues which, perhaps, cannot be comprehensively dealt with during the PGCE year, but without which we might feel the initial training course was excessively narrow. Here we would place such issues as multi-cultural education, gender, counselling and pastoral care, and minority group interests.

We think special educational needs (SEN) is related to the three aspects in that it has implications for immediate rôles; it can be part of the teacher's widening conception of his or her rôle and has many affinities with several 'minority' group issues. In combination, these relationships suggest an important place for SEN components within initial training and beyond that, given the current process of changing conceptions of special needs and the restructuring of delivery services, they can be seen as creating opportunities for training institutions to orient the new teacher towards becoming part of the change process.

This orientation could for example, emphasise the importance of accepting that special needs do not entail separate provision and that handicap derives as much from the way children are perceived and treated as from their mental or physical impairment. At the same time students need to feel competent and confident in their ability to deal with problems when they arise in the ordinary classroom. What shall it profit the tutor if he imparts an appropriate philosophy on "integration" but the student feels so insecure with actual pupils with learning difficulties that effective action is not matched to ideological commitment.

78

One more pressure on training institutions?

From the inside of training institutions, SEN looks like yet another of the increasing demands on time and resources alongside making primary school teachers subject specialists, providing computing experience and all the other expectations derived from the 'Teaching Quality' paper and pressure from a legion of vested interest groups, all convinced that multi-cultural needlework, parental control over the curriculum or driver education for the pre-school pupil is the panacea.

Those with experience of PGCE courses will know the degree of change that has taken place with the shift of emphasis from 'Foundation' disciplines to the pre-eminence currently enjoyed by subject specialisms and classroom practice. This change will be accelerated by the impact of 'Teaching Quality' paper and those of us who wish to advocate a place of SEN on our courses will have a task to justify its place not simply as a fashionable response to current interests and enthusiasms, but as an enduring and we believe, essential component.

The context into which SEN courses are being injected is a fluid one, and this is our opportunity to make our case, although in a number of institutions, the case has been made and accepted. We should be somewhat wary of pretending that SEN courses can offer a secure, unambiguous or consensual knowledge territory which can be handed over with certainty or confidence. Research on SEN courses shows how under the one banner of SEN a motley army has gathered. These vile and ragged foils consist of courses labelled 'identification of SEN'; 'language problems'; 'support services'; 'behaviour problems' and 'learning difficulties'. There does not appear to be a general consensus about what should be the orientation and content of initial training SEN courses. Further variations exist between length of course (10 to 80 hours); the number of tutors involved (ranging from the solitary institutional expert to quite large teams of up to fifteen tutors) and whether or not there is or should be some kind of practicum associated with the course. We are all 'for' SEN courses, but is there a 'core' curriculum? We can blandly agree with the ACSET recommendations, but can we agree on the content of 'how to identify special educational needs'?

If for some institutions SEN is a major agendum item, for others it is 'any other business' and for a few even 'apologies for absence', we will need to argue the rightful place of such courses. Earlier it was suggested SEN was related to the primary tasks of initial training so we have no doubt that SEN should figure in these courses and from personal experience (which we know is shared by many other tutors) that there is a significant percentage of PGCE students who are enthusiastic about this part of their work. Paradoxically, we believe the most pressing argument for SEN in initial training is *not only for what it may achieve for the child with special needs,   but for what it can achieve for initial training itself*,   (e.g. concern for each individual, matching teaching to patterns of ability and disability, integration of 'minority' members, close cooperation with parents, effective use of support services, careful monitoring of progress, etc.)

Content, timing and delivery

Having, we hope suggested that SEN courses have a place in initial training, we need to think about the content, timing and delivery style of such courses. Here the problem can be expressed quite simply: it is what to leave out.   It is perfectly possible to generate content that is interesting. We can provide courses which alphabetically include autism, brain damage, cystic fibrosis, dyslexia, enuresis, Frostig, German measles, handedness, idiopathic epilepsy, juvenile delinquency, kyphosis, laterality, mongolism, neurosis, oligophrenia, perthes disease, quotients, retrolentula fibroplasia, Seguin form boards, tactile acuity, Underwood Report, Vineland scales, Wechster sub-tests, X-rays, Y chromosomes and Z scores.   The problem is not one of shortage of material, but of ideas about the *appropriate criteria* for the selection and organisation of content and experiences which are appropriate for students at a *particular stage of professional development* which will help them in fulfilling immediate and future rôles in partnership with current developments.

Colin Smith's research probe into the attitudes of students at Birmingham brings out very clearly the degree of student involvement with SEN issues.   It also helps with the development of criteria for content selection (Smith, 1983). Content should be based on the probability of its relevance to recent student experience. Colin Smith found that over half of the students, training as secondary subject specialists, had part of their teaching practice timetable - allocated to work with groups, specifically designated by the school as being for children with difficulties in learning.   They felt that they coped adequately with teaching pupils who had problems in reading, writing, spelling and mathematics, but would welcome more preparation for this type of work. Most subject method courses did not deal with the particular problems of less able children and the students placed high on their list of SEN priorities a deeper understanding of ways to help pupils with learning difficulties and advice about the management of difficult and disruptive pupils.   The second criterion we suggest is for content which focuses upon the most commonly encountered learning and behavioural problems, and thirdly, the discussion of practice, policy and perspectives to take place within those contexts which have immediate relevance for students, (e.g. how to help a child with reading before dipping the toe into the murky pond of dyslexia; behaviour disorder in the classroom before autism; mixed ability teaching in secondary schools before interesting visits to CHE). Colin Smith's students, who had taken both a general course on children with special needs and a more specific option on teaching slow learners emphasised that whilst the former was interesting the latter was immediately useful. They wanted to know about different disabilities and how social attitudes can help create handicap. However, their immediate concern was with classroom management and organisation, coping with misbehaviour and adapting curriculum materials. These matters are not, of course, the exclusive concern of special education but for this group of students these were the issues which they thought should be thoroughly tackled in this part of the course.

There is a debate on whether SEN courses in initial training should be of the 'awareness' variety, or based on practical classroom skills or some uneasy mixture of both. Similarly, there is a debate as to whether SEN courses are provided as self-contained capsules or integrated into the training programmes as a whole, and there are arguments over the balance between courses, between lectures/seminars and school-based experience.

An example of an awareness course is given below.

For all students: a short 10 hour programme: introductory and general in nature:

(a) provide an awareness of children with special needs: characteristics, frequency, distribution, causation and major patterns of identification, support and provision

(b) exemplified through case studies, contacts with teachers, psychologists, social workers, education welfare officers.

(c) providing examples of effective integration and mainstreaming

(d) stressing the rôle of all teachers in meeting special needs

(e) knowledge of the support services

81

(f) resources; selected readings; curriculum materials; diagnostic tests; remedial programmes; adaptions of curriculum materials etc.

A more classroom based course for Primary PGCE students consisted of the following:-

early identification of learning and behaviour difficulties; individual and group assessment; diagnosis of reading and language problems; remedial maths programmes; visual and auditory perceptual skills; child study of special needs; working with small groups of slow learners; adapting curriculum materials to suit readability levels and differing conceptual levels; working with parents; team teaching.

These are actual examples of current practice and they are not offered here as model models; what they have in common is that they are both offered to students as self-contained capsules of instruction. They both reinforce the concept of SEN as a distinct and separate entity for the rest of the training programme. Perhaps marginally better than no in-put, but not necessarily the ideal pattern. There are wide-spread differences in the timing of SEN courses within initial training. Some tutors believe it is worthwhile to delay SEN in-put until after students have had some experience with mainstream groups.

Integrating special needs in training

The H.M.I. discussion document, *Teaching in Schools* (1983) in the summary of its main recommendations has this to say

"All courses of training should include practical experience and knowledge of class management and control; knowledge of the variety that constitutes the full range of pupils in terms of behaviour, social background and culture; experience and knowledge of the level of performance appropriate for differing ages, abilities and backgrounds ..." (P17)

It does not mention SEN but states that students should be familiar with "... the practice of assessment; individual differences in the way in which children learn (and) with understanding of some of the more common learning difficulties ..."

In other words, initial training should as a *part* of its

general preparation of students incorporate the study of differences, individual diversity of styles of learning, special needs and developmental levels as part of the training programme. As such this view rejects the conception of SEN courses as distinct and separate and places the responsibility for the meeting of special needs in training on the whole training institution. The best pattern of integrated training is still being worked out, but the ACSET recommendation on subject specialisms underlines the involvement of a wider range of tutors than just the token 'special needs' tutor.

One of the key issues in initial training and SEN is the part to be played by subject specialists and by institutional experts in the field of special needs. Where training institutions have members of staff who are acknowledged experts in the field of learning disabilities it will be natural for the institution's efforts in incorporating a special needs component in initial training to be focused on such staff members. This can mean that such individuals will be obliged to carry a heavy teaching-organising load if all students are to have some SEN exposure at some time during their course. The simplest organisational response to such pressure is to mount short intensive courses for large groups.

While economies of scale have to be entertained during a period when most training institutions are experiencing pressures on human and financial resources the 'mass' lecture format is hardly ideal for the discussion of learning difficulties or the problems of behaviour management in classrooms. As well as presenting institutions with new issues with respect to the content of SEN courses there are a number of problems on the delivery side. Similar issues arise on the valuable contribution to SEN courses which can be made by visiting speakers who can bring specialist professional expertise and the reality of current practice to enhance internal contributions. If we are to work effectively with small groups of students shall we be obliged to provide each group with its quota of educational psychologists, social workers and heads of remedial or special needs departments? At the present time the demand for SEN courses has been made without a great deal of regard for the consequential impact of this requirement on institutional resources. It is an easy matter for the Secretary of State for Education to hold over training institutions the threat that failure to deliver appropriate SEN courses could result in the withdrawal of official approval of training certification, and another to match this demand for additional training input with appropriate resources. This has parallels with central government's failure to match the resource implications of the Warnock Report.

83

It may be that the way forward in difficult time is to apply to SEN initial training courses some of the features which we would hope would be strong value component within such courses. For example, we would see SEN courses emphasising the significance of individual differences, paced learning, resource-based learning and the generation of high levels of motivation. The response of several training institutions in this area has been the generation of resource 'packs' to complement internal input and supplemented by the growing amount of film and video material available from the Open University, the ILEA, and other local authorities such as Coventry.

Awareness, skills and attitudes

The popularity of 'awareness' type SEN courses in initial training may be in part due to the pressures of attempting to meet the minimalist requirements which the current climate appears to demand. However, Colin Smith's inquiry seems to suggest that as far as students are concerned 'awareness' courses do not appear to meet *their* special needs. His students were clear that beyond awareness there was a demand for courses which could assist with their willingness to offer help to slow learning and other children with special educational needs. We feel that at an early stage in the training programme there should be a wide-ranging introductory course which seeks to create a climate in which there is a general expectation that as an integral part of the teacher's role (whatever the subject specialism) the role embraces a professional concern for children with learning difficulties (as outlined earlier). We see this not as an exclusive area devoted to 'special needs' but including a number of 'minority group' areas to which the teachers in training will have their attention drawn. Multi-cultural education is the clearest example of another area where 'awareness' issues arise.

If initial training is to have an impact on school practice and policy in the area of special needs such introductory and orienting courses by themselves will not be effective unless they are complemented by courses which focus upon curriculum and classroom issues as indicated by the type of input we have called 'skill' courses.

The impact of SEN on training

We see the incorporation of both awareness and skill courses being relatively easy within the context of initial training for Primary school teachers. In the sense that Primary education has built-in values which accept the conception of mixed-ability grouping, individual learning and a concern for the fundamentals of learning. There may be a somewhat greater difficulty in getting subject specialists to accept that their training concerns embrace the whole ability range within the school population. This brings us to an area where we feel the impact of SEN courses can have a profound effect upon the nature of initial training. Not only will the subject specialists be encouraged to widen the scope of their concerns to the whole ability range and to seek ways of making the curriculum accessible to all pupils, this must also inevitably bring with it a closer association between the content of the subject specialist course and fundamental issues concerning learning, concept formation, language and learning motivation and attitudes which will be shared by other subject specialists. In other words there will be an institutional orientation towards a deeper appreciation of the interaction between pupil performance and teaching. (Clunies-Ross, 1983)

Such changes are not going to be accomplished overnight. Neither should it be expected that specialists can achieve this change without some in-service training or support. Here we see a distinctive role for the 'special needs' expert. This could be by the experienced special educator being included in the work of the subject specialist group or, and this would be our preference, by being a resource and a consultant to specialist colleagues. In this way we believe the practical requirements of meeting special needs in schools will be better met by the combination of general awareness courses and by specific input integrated into the warp and weft of the students' main professional concerns. If the main thrust of this argument is taken, the institutional implications are considerable, for it suggests that the matter of meeting special needs cannot be compartmentalised into either token awareness offerings or left to the discretion or whim of the subject specialist tutor. It becomes a matter for institutional policy-making, planning and resource allocation.

The ACSET report suggest that this process might be assisted through a combination of national and regional seminars and conferences, in-house programmes for staff development, wider dissemination of good practice in initial training and new staff appointments enhancing expertise in the area of special educational needs. Financial constraints and competing demands for limited resources make it unlikely that these proposals can be effected on a scale sufficient to ensure an immediate and widespread change in approach. Most institutions will continue to draw on the experience and expertise of a limited number of tutors usually already heavily involved with in-service training.

With all their limitations, present SEN courses can ensure that all students receive some help and guidance about how to deal with pupils, who have difficulties in learning. Opting for a policy of wider involvement, without adequate resources for retraining or support, could mean worse not better provision. For the moment, at least, tutors with personal experience of working with children with special needs, may still be best employed in passing it directly to students, whilst also taking every opportunity to work alongside subject specialist colleagues, particularly in relation to preparation for teaching practice.

Last point: the H.M.I. proposals emphasise the essentially classroom based and practical nature of training. That would be fine except for the fact that as a basis for training SEN has a rather insecure knowledge base. Special needs is an area characterised by enormous diversity of practice, provision, policy implementation: there are opposing camps of diagnosticians and 'whole school' curriculum believers; behaviour modifiers confront humanistic psychologists; prescriptive teachers disagree with precision teachers and the whole area is replete with sociological and philosophical debates.

We cannot accept that in the name of initial training and the desire to improve classroom practice we should shield students from the full force of these controversial issues. SEN courses can be relevant and practical, they can be located within an integrated training structure, but they will be intellectually vigorous and stimulating, precisely to the degree that they put these controversial issues before the student. Nothing could be more fruitful for the generation of demanding and exciting courses than for students to be part of a debate where strong views are held and where students can come to a personal view rather than be handed an institutional prescription: such prescriptions are so often marked 'valium'.

Chapter Seven

POST-EXPERIENCE TRAINING

Klaus Wedell

One of the main points which emerges from previous chapters is that educational provision for children's special needs can no longer be considered in isolation. Provision for children's special needs has to be seen as part of the system of education as a whole. The further training of teachers to meet the special educational needs has therefore also to be considered in context. This context includes central and local government policy as far as this exists, teacher training establishments, and the education and other services concerned, quite apart from the children and their various needs. For the purpose of this chapter, one has to select a starting point within the complex pattern of interdependence. It seems appropriate to consider first our current understanding of the nature of children's special educational needs, since the ultimate criterion of teacher education must be represented by whether or not these needs are met. The pattern of service delivery appropriate to provide for these needs is the next consideration along with the roles and functions of the personnel who provide the services. The contribution which the in-service education of teachers may make will then be considered in relation to these roles and functions. This, in turn, will raise the issue of the relationship between Local Education Authorities (LEAs), their services, and the providers of in-service education both within the LEAs and within the Institutions of Higher Education (IHEs) whether in the public or University sector.

Changes are occurring in all these aspects of the topic. Our concepts of children's needs are changing, LEA provision is changing, and IHEs are changing - or even ceasing to exist. To attempt to consider the role of in-service education in the midst of such a fluid situation will therefore not be an easy task.

Special Educational Needs

It is now well known that through its definition of Special Educational Needs the 1981 Education Act established the relative and interactive view of the children's needs which had been gaining acceptance over the last ten years or so. By affirming the Warnock Report's (1978) rejection of any clear-cut distinction between the handicapped and the non-handicapped, the drafters of the Act did away with the categories which had hitherto formed the basis for educational provision and established the concept of the 'continuum of special educational need'. The continuum of special need is already represented by the way in which reference is now being made to the '2%', the '18%' and even the '40%' of pupils with special needs, although even such references fail to focus on needs rather than children. The formulation of 'ordinary' and 'special' provision in the Act also, by implication, affirmed a relative and interactive view of special educational needs. It is clear that the full import of this view of need is only gradually being registered both at the central and at the local government level. Another attempt to grasp the implications of the conceptual change is represented by the way schools have been required by the DES to report on Forms 7 and 7M the information about pupils for whom statements have been made. The central concept underlying this formulation involves distinctions between the levels of curricula which the children are regarded as requiring.

It has been clearly stated that provision should be made for children from birth to 19 years, but neither local nor central government has followed this through to policy or provision.

Service Delivery

The new legislation's affirmation of the relative and interactive view of special educational need produces problems for administrators. Children may require special provision in one setting but not in another, at one time, but not at another. This ambiguity is, of course, not new, but the previous procedures for identifying pupils with special needs at least made it possible officially, to disregard it. Some may suppose that the new statementing procedure offers a standard means of identifying pupils with more severe forms of special need, but this is neither implied by the wording of the Act, nor evident from the contrasting statementing policies of different LEAs.

The abolition of handicap categories contributes to the administrators' problems because of the difficulty it presents in characterising special provision. It is no comfort to point out that provision which was previously subsumed within a particular category, often in fact, differed considerably. Furthermore, these differences were recognised and acted upon by those concerned with meeting children's needs.

It is not surprising that some of those concerned with planning the provision of special educational resources, have come to question whether it is appropriate or even relevant, to do this solely on the basis of the number of *individually* identified children. Instead, they propose that services should be conceived as directed at the range of degree and nature of educational need among children in an area. While this may conform to the view of special need described above, it does not relieve the administrators' problem since they are still left with the hopeless search for a basis on which to estimate service and staffing requirements.

I propose, none the less, to use such a model of service delivery for the purpose of identifying the roles and functions of personnel concerned with meeting children's special needs. The nature of such a model has been set out in other chapters. It is sufficient therefore to make some general points, and then to consider the likely roles and functions of the constituent groups of personnel. It is evident that, within this model, any individual pupil's degree of participation in the generally provided curriculum will vary according to the judgement of those involved, as to whether the pupil is making acceptable progress. The allocation to the pupil of a range of additional resources will follow from decisions based on this judgement, and may result in the pupil being segregated to a greater or lesser extent in terms of time or place from the general body of pupils.

Support for the pupil starts in the ordinary classroom, and will involve a range of resource personnel who can support the ordinary teacher, or who may provide direct support for pupils within the classroom, the school or elsewhere. Support is, of course, not only provided by teachers of various kinds, but also by personnel from medical, social, psychological and other services. Similarly, the model also involves a recognition of the contribution which parents and members of the community can make, quite apart from the way in which pupils can help each other. Within this overall model of service delivery, one can identify the following group of education personnel, whose function and roles imply a requirement for in-service education.

1. 'Ordinary' classroom teachers. It is evident that the ordinary classroom teacher has to have a sufficiently explicit and detailed understanding of the curriculum, to be able to use this to notice when pupils are having difficulty in making progress. Teachers need also to have a range of methods for helping such children, and sufficient familiarity

with the commoner forms of disability which may limit a child's response to teaching. Finally, teachers need ways of recognising if their own efforts to support a child are inadequate, and how to obtain access to extra help. Clearly, these aspects of the ordinary teacher's role and function should be covered in initial training, but it is evident that, at least up to now, this has not been adequately provided, and LEAs are engaging in a range of 'awareness' and other in-service education measures to support teachers.

2. 'Resource' teachers. Regardless of the extent to which pupils may or may not be segregated in order to receive special educational help, teachers will be needed whose role it is to have a level and nature of teaching competence and understanding to enable them to provide such help. This function may involve support for teachers and others who have day-to-day care of children, it may involve additional direct support for the pupils, or it may involve personal responsibility for the education of the pupils in units or special schools. To fulfil this role, such resource teachers will have to be able to offer a degree of expertise and specialist knowledge which is sufficient to make a significant contribution to supporting ordinary teachers and others, and to helping a pupil make progress.

It is obvious that any one resource teacher cannot be expected to have the competencies and knowledge required to help the whole range of children with special needs, and consequently, that resource teachers will have to have particular specialisms. In the past, these specialisms tended to be linked to particular handicaps or types of service (e.g. remedial teachers). The form which such specialism should now take is an open question, but it is generally agreed that help has to be offered in the context of the curriculum. Furthermore, such resource teachers should have access to the normal range of promotion, and thus to meet the requirements associated with this. The recent ACSET recommendation that all resource teachers should have prior training and experience as ordinary teachers, is very much influenced by this consideration. It is evident therefore, that the kinds of specialisation required of resource teachers will have to be acquired through in-service education.

3. 'Designated' teachers in ordinary schools. The role of these teachers is suggested in Circular 3/83. The stated intention is that, in each school, there should be a teacher with managerial responsibility for ensuring that the special educational needs of pupils were identified, and that relevant resource personnel and services were mobilised to support the child. In order to do this, designated teachers were expected to have a basic knowledge about the means of identifying

children's special needs, and of initiating first-line curricular modifications to meet these needs. They were also required to have a knowledge of the relevant support services available within the LA. The managerial functions of designated teachers would differ with the size of the school, and correspondingly also between primary and secondary schools, but it is clear that they were not perceived to have the specialist role assigned to resource teachers.

4. In a service delivery model which requires a response to children's special needs in the whole of 'ordinary' provision, there is obviously a need for those with broader managerial responsibility in schools, or with subject responsibility, to have an awareness of aspects relevant to special educational need. This represents one among a number of factors which such personnel have to take into consideration, but for which they require additional knowledge and competence. Heads and others with managerial responsibility, and subject specialists, have their respective in-service training provision, and aspects of relevance to special needs will have to be included.

5. Special Education Advisers and Special Education Administrators. It is evident that the roles and functions of those with professional and administrative responsibilities for pupils with special needs within an LEA require a commensurate level of competence and knowledge. This applies particularly to their responsibility for formulating an LEA's policy and for developing the LEA's provision.

6. Non-teaching aides. Most LEAs employ a range of non-teaching aides in order to make it possible for teachers to cope with the number of demands made on them in their attempts to meet children's special needs, whether in ordinary classrooms, or in some form of special provision. The contribution which personnel of this kind make is very considerable, and it is evident that their roles and functions can be greatly enhanced with appropriate in-service training.

The above account of some of the roles and functions of personnel can apply similarly to 'resource' models of service delivery, and to service models which provide for special needs mainly through special schools and units. The common factor among the roles and functions described, is that they are not ones for which initial teacher training can be regarded as a sufficient preparation, and which therefore represent demands for in-service education. One important group of personnel whose training needs have not been mentioned above, are those whose primary function is to provide the in-service education itself. This group includes the relevant staff of IHEs, and also those who act as 'master teachers' in those schools and LEAs who employ teachers in this capacity. Although the staff responsible in IHEs may have followed a variety of career patterns, they themselves will have required appropriate advanced training. The priorities of such training has to be included in any plan for a constellation of in-service education provision.

To summarise; the new concepts of special educational need are altering views about the nature and organisation of service delivery required to meet children's needs. These models of service delivery make additional demands on teachers in ordinary schools, and require a range of support personnel with relevant knowledge and competence. This knowledge and competence is different in kind and level for ordinary teachers and for the various types of resource personnel, but broadly includes the following aspects:

(a) an understanding of the nature of special educational need in the context of the relative and interactive view of 'need',

(b) strategies for identifying and responding to special educational needs, and the knowledge and competence to do this,

(c) an understanding of resource management needed for (b) and, particularly for resource personnel.

(d) competencies in influencing the attitude of others, and in passing on knowledge and skills to those with day-to-day responsibility for children with special needs. Those concerned particularly with policy development and innovation will require the level of competence necessary for this.

How Can In-Service Education Support Service Delivery?

The function of in-service education is to provide personnel with the above knowledge and competence - both to fulfil existing service delivery demands, and to develop services. This immediately raises the question as to who has the necessary knowledge and competence to offer such education?

There is no doubt that a considerable resource of personnel already exists in services. These include people at all levels, from classroom teachers to advisory and administrative personnel. They differ, of course, in the extent to which they have an explicit as well as an implicit awareness of the knowledge and competence they possess, and consequently of the extent to which they are in a position to pass on their expertise. They definitely also differ in their ability to communicate their expertise to others.

An overriding constraint on their ability to contribute to in-service education is, of course, likely to be the fact that their duties do not allow time for this. However, most LEAs have some personnel who provide, at the least, occasional in-service courses at Teachers' Centres, and some contribute to courses in IHEs. Similarly, an increasing number of schools use their specialist teachers for school-based in-service education.

Many IHEs, of course, have lecturers who are responsible for running courses, although the recent cuts have severely reduced the staff for this in many IHEs to the point where some courses have been closed. The extent to which lecturers in the IHEs have practical competencies of relevance to current modes of service delivery for special educational needs varies considerably and the pressures on them leave little time to maintain and develop their competencies in direct field work. The contraction of IHE staff resources has meant that there has been little scope for recent recruitment from 'field' personnel, although in a few instances, some attempts have and are being made to create joint appointments between IHEs and LEAs. IHE staff frequently also contribute to LEA and school-based in-service courses.

In general, it has to be acknowledged that there is not anything like a sufficient body of personnel who have both the practical and theoretical requirements to provide the scale and level of in-service education demanded in the present situation. There is a larger resource of personnel who have *either* some of the practical *or* some of the theoretical requirements. In addition to this unsatisfactory state of affairs, there is a more pervasive and underlying problem - namely the rarity in LEAs of any explicit and coordinated policy on in-service education with regard to the development of special needs services. Teachers tend to be chosen for courses at IHEs as a 'reward' for long service, rather than to prepare for a contribution to the development of service delivery. Teachers returning from courses to their schools are teased about their luck in having 'time off', and are told in no uncertain terms by their colleagues to keep their recently acquired 'new-fangled ideas' to themselves. Studies abound about the lack of use which teachers who have completed in-service courses make of the knowledge and competencies they acquired.

Within most LEAs in-service education is supported in a somewhat haphazard way, frequently by allocating resources allocated to the particular initiatives of individuals or groups of staff. More recently, in response to the promptings of the Warnock Report, LEA staff concerned with special needs have initiated various forms of 'awareness' courses for teaching staff in ordinary schools, and some of such schemes have been adequately resourced, comprehensively conceived and effectively implemented.   If any significant impact is to be made on the development of LEA services for children with special needs, there is no doubt that service delivery will have to be based on a clearly articulated policy on in-service education.   Such a policy will, of course, have to be planned within the constraints of the limited financial resources available to LEAs, but the awareness of the pervasiveness of special educational need among the '20%' or '40%' of pupils implies the scale on which the share of existing resources should be allocated.   To maximise the effectiveness of such investment, some LEAs are already implementing a 'pyramid' system of training, by which those on courses at higher levels are given the responsibility of passing what they have learned on to others, and so on.   At each level, personnel have, of course, to be given time and other necessary resources to play their part effectively in a 'pyramid'.   Such a level of conceptualisation, planning, and indeed initial commitment by LEAs is, however, relatively rare.   Some LEAs are, for example, expecting teachers who have attended the one-term Circular 3/83 courses to take responsibility for providing in-service education at a level which is quite inappropriate to the level of qualification which the courses are intended to provide. Other LEAs are expecting to influence policy and practice within schools, through teachers whose status is quite inappropriate to achieve this.

It is evident that, if any LEA policy on in-service education is to have a chance of being effective, it must be based also on sound managerial principles.   These principles need to apply both to the provision of in-service education, and to the application of its intended outcome.   A number of factors determine the extent to which effective policy implementation can be achieved.   The need for an initial commitment to policy formulation as such has already been mentioned.   Another consideration relates to the effective use of available and potential trainers. Training staff exist in both LEAs and in IHEs, but there is surprisingly little coordination of their training   contributions at any systematic level, considering the extent to which the relative preponderance of practical and theoretical expertise in each could complement the other.   To some extent this is analogous to the unsatisfactory state of affairs on initial teacher education, as has been recognised in recent government pronouncements.   It seems quite clear however, that such a state of affairs is quite unacceptable in the area of special educational need, where the interaction of theory and practice is central to the subject matter.   A divorce between the training of personnel and practice would, by analogy, be inconceivable in medicine.

There are, of course, a host of problems facing those who would attempt to coordinate the in-service education contribution of the available personnel in IHEs and LEAs, - even in the case of staffs of colleges run by LEAs. Courses in IHEs serve students from a wide range of LEAs and many serve students from overseas. IHEs are largely concerned with award bearing courses, which have their particular entry requirements and formats. Existing secondment regulations determine the length and form of courses also. While LEAs are normally generous in providing practical placements for students attending IHE courses, LEAs' shortage of key competent and responsible personnel make them reluctant to permit them to allocate time to participate in IHE courses.

Problems also affect the extent to which the practical placements of teachers on in-service courses can be incorporated into the normal teaching service. This is in interesting contrast to 'practice teaching' in initial teacher education, where students' participation in the ordinary pattern of teaching services is quite accepted. In in-service education, the need for student teachers to have extensive experience of work in services for children with special needs is fully accepted, but there is little recognition that this could actually be incorporated into the provision of service delivery. For example, it is certainly not generally accepted that the contribution which teachers on in-service courses make during their placements, could be reckoned to justify the secondment of an LEA staff member to participate in an IHE in-service course for some corresponding proportion of time.

The organisation of full and part-time course attendance is also surrounded by problems although such a combined pattern might be particularly suitable for in-service education for special needs teachers. The existing administrative requirements of both LEAs and IHEs makes a more flexible approach to such organisation difficult. For IHEs, it would imply a modular approach to course organisation. However, the feasibility of this is being investigated in an experimental project in NW England. A multitude of factors make patterns of combined and part-time attendance at courses difficult. For example, there is a gross discrepancy between the financial support to universities of full and part-time students, which would make the staffing of mixed courses practically impossible. There are recent proposals from a UGC committee to correct this discrepancy. LEAs also would have problems in committing themselves to ensuring that a teacher could follow a pattern of full and part-time attendance, leading up to the completion of an award-bearing course.

These problems represent only a small selection of those that seem to militate against the coordination of LEA and IHE in-service endeavours. The problems which have been described concern mainly the provision of courses in IHEs. These courses however, play a central part in the development of services, since they are intended to provide the higher levels of qualification, and so to provide the personnel who can initiate the various 'pyramids' of in-service education within LEAs.

One should, perhaps, also acknowledge that those responsible for in-service education in LEAs and in IHEs do not always regard each other as potential collaborators in the provision and development of courses. There is frequently a communication gap between these two groups of people. This may arise from no more than the pressure of work under which each operates. It may however, reflect in some instances a mutual ascription of contrary views about the role and function of in-service education, which may or may not be based on fact. In caricature, the LEA person sees the IHE person as one who regards the purpose of in-service education to be the enhancement of the teacher's personal intellectual development towards theoretical ideas which, even if they had practical implications, were none-the-less bound to be impossible to implement. The IHE person, on the other hand, is caricatured as being intent on using in-service education as a means of inducting staff into prescribed procedures, without any requirement for understanding or evaluating these. Needless to say, such extreme ascriptions probably do not actually exist, but they do occur in moderated forms, and no doubt some grounds exist, which make them not entirely without foundation. All the more reason therefore, for those concerned with in-service education in IHEs and LEAs to get together, in order to establish a common basis for communication, and for planning an effective policy for meeting the pressing need for effective in-service education provision. Furthermore both groups need to recognise that the other may provide ideas for innovation and development.

It is interesting to note that, increasingly, communication and collaboration is developing. The provision of modular in-service courses in the NW is an example of LEA/IHE collaboration. A number of the Circular 3/83 courses also are organised on a close collaboration between IHEs and LEAs. In one course, for example, this collaboration started with the initial planning of the course, which involved a group of those staff in several IHEs and LEAs who were responsible for special needs in-service education in the SE of England. The selection of teachers for the courses was left to LEA personnel, but both the heads of the seconded teachers' schools, and the LEA special needs advisers were required to make written commitments to support the work of the teachers during and after the course. The teachers, for their part, were required, as part of the course, to develop and carry out a project which contributed to their schools' support of pupils with special educational needs. The course organisers have regular meetings with the heads of the schools and the LEA advisers, to monitor and develop the content and organisation of the course. It is significant that the above example concerns a non-award bearing course, where some of the usual academic organisational constraints did not apply. None the less, these and similar instances offer indications of the way in which the interrelationship between in-service education and service delivery can be established.

Types of In-Service Education Courses

In line with the rationale adopted in this paper, in-service courses will be discussed in the context of the personnel they are intended to serve.

Teachers in ordinary schools. Initial teacher education is the subject of another chapter and so will not be dealt with here. The Warnock Report, however, identified the need to provide 'awareness' courses for teachers already in schools, to raise the level of their contribution to pupils with special needs in ordinary classes. LEAs have attempted to meet this need in a variety of ways. Some LEAs have devised a short part-time in-service programme which is repeated in different parts of an Authority's area. These courses have been largely concerned with informing teachers about the nature of various forms of disability, and about the support services available. Such courses have been arranged in a repeatable form, either through the organisation of a 'travelling circus' of staff, or sometimes through the production of audio-visual materials which form a central course resource. The DES has itself produced a package of this kind.

Another type of approach has focussed on increasing the teacher's initial identification and intervention skills. The Coventry SNAP programme is an example of this, which has been adopted by a number of other LEAs also. This programme is firmly based on an objective oriented approach to teaching, and aims to introduce teachers to the need to formulate at least the mastery aspects of their curriculum in a framework of progressive objects. Teachers are then shown how this framework can be used to assess the learning needs of pupils, and also to indicate appropriately sized steps for pupils' further progress. Organisationally, the SNAP courses involve a pyramid teaching approach, with a focus on school-based in-service education by teachers who have attended preparation courses.

The above represent two examples of awareness courses. The variety of approaches adopted by different LEAs is very wide, but surveys indicate that almost all LEAs are attempting to make some kind of provision.

Resource teachers. As mentioned in the first section of this paper, these teachers are intended to provide the key specialist resource for pupils with special needs. The Warnock Report recommended that such a teaching force should be formed through the provision of recognised qualifications. The ACSET Working Party recommends that these qualifications require one year full-time courses or the equivalent. A number of such courses exist at present and lead to Diploma or post-experience graduate qualifications at Colleges and Universities.

They differ considerably in the level of knowledge and competence aimed for, and in the extent to which they focus on serving a particular aspect of special need. In general, courses have up to now been mainly grouped into those offering a broadly based introduction to the main range of learning and behaviour problems, and those which aim to prepare teachers to work with children in one of the main erstwhile categories of handicap. This diversity also applies to the two examples of distance teaching offered at this level. The OU is planning to extend its current special needs unit into a general course, and a specialist course for teachers of the visually impaired is provided by the University of Birmingham. A small number of courses in IHEs with a range of staff, have developed courses which offer a core component of study, linked to opportunities for specialisation in one or other aspects of special needs teaching. The ACSET Working Party Report supports such an approach on a number of grounds:

(a) the rôles and functions which are required of resource teachers demand a specialist level of training,

(b) however, it is generally recognised that there is an extensive common element in the knowledge and competencies required by resource teachers in different specialisms,

(c) teachers working in, or preparing to work in, different specialisms benefit from opportunities to exchange views and compare issues,

(d) the nature of specialisation required in the special needs field is likely to be one of its most rapidly developing aspects, so that this form of in-service organisation can allow for the flexibility which will be required.

The common core for these courses needs to prepare teachers for the problem solving strategies mentioned in the earlier section. To achieve this, teachers require a level of understanding of theoretical models derived from the main relevant areas such as educational and developmental psychology, curriculum study and sociology. The core element also should include a knowledge of service delivery systems and the legislative context. A particular focus on resource management is needed as has already been indicated above. The role these teachers will have to play in initiating pyramid systems of in-service education at all levels indicates that the consultation and other relevant competencies will have to form a part of the core component.

The basis on which the specialisation components of those courses should be chosen raises a very problematic issue, on which opinions are likely to vary considerably. This is clearly an aspect in which a match will have to be achieved between the courses and LEA patterns of service delivery. Since any one course is likely to recruit teachers from a number of LEAs such matching will present considerable difficulty. It may be, therefore, that this aspect should be one in which courses should organise a high level of LEA collaboration in in-service education. Such collaboration would, of course, require that LEAs could offer examples of exemplary practice for training purposes.

The interaction of theory and practice forms a central element in these recognised qualification courses, and indicates the need for collaboration between IHEs and LEAs both organisationally, and at the level of personal contact between LEA and IHE staff concerned. It is also important that the key role of resource teachers is considered in the investment of item allocated to their attendance at the courses. Half-hearted commitment by LEAs to quality of in-service education at this level will be a correspondingly poor investment. Secondment to these courses has to derive from clearly articulated policies on the development of service delivery.

Special education advisers, IHE lectures and others concerned with policy and service delivery development

The Warnock Report recommended that Masters level courses should be available to prepare personnel for posts involving responsibility at this level. In fact, few Masters courses exist at present, and LEAs have in general not given priority to seconding staff to them. Consequently, teachers have more frequently attended part-time versions of these courses. The few courses which exist tend to have been set up relatively recently, and their aims appear to differ very considerably. Some courses appear to offer slightly higher levels of general study in the special needs area, while others allow teachers varying levels of specialisation. If these courses are to meet the needs of this level of personnel the content and nature of courses, and the level of study will have to be carefully matched. Furthermore, the inter-relationship between theory and practice in the content of these courses represents a key issue, since LEAs' perceptions of Masters' level courses often assume an inordinate emphasis on theory. There seems no doubt, however, that Masters courses offer an opportunity for a high level study of practice and the way this informs theory, as well as the other way about.

Since so few Masters courses are yet available, and the number of trained personnel are in any case so small, most LEAs currently choose recognised qualification courses in seconding personnel at the advisory level. Similarly, special needs staff in IHEs by no means all have qualifications at Masters level - at least not qualifications in special needs.

Designated Teachers. The recognition of teachers with these roles and functions is a relatively recent development, and has been closely associated with the DES initiative set out in Circular 3/83. This represents a rare example of DES involvement in developing service delivery linked with in-service education. Aspects of these courses have already been mentioned in the foregoing. Although the circular specifies the foci required in the content of these courses, LEAs have widely differing views of the roles and functions required of the teachers they second. There seems no doubt that the courses are making a contribution to the teachers who attend them, but the practical realisation of the specifica- tions in the circular has demonstrated the problems of implementing centrally formulated policy.

The courses have been developed in very different ways, particularly in their organisation. As was mentioned above, a considerable degree of collaboration between LEAs and IHEs has been engendered. Some IHEs are also considering the incorporation of the courses into a modular version of recognised qualifications.

Teachers' Aides. The particular roles and functions allocated to teachers' aides differ widely, but some LEAs are recognis- ing their potential contribution, and are providing local courses for them. It seems clear that, if resource teachers for children with severe forms of special needs are to fulfil a consultancy role outside their schools and units, teachers' aides may play a particular part in contributing to the continuity of care the children require. The varied nature of these posts makes it essential that in-service education is closely matched to the service provided, and correspondingly that the courses should be run by individuals.

Apart from the above courses geared to the supply of personnel at various levels, there is clearly a need to provide courses which enable staff to be kept up-to-date with developments in the area; to enable staff to transfer from one form of specialisation to another; and to acquire particular further levels of specialisation. Courses of this kind are currently offered on a limited scale and in a rather uncoordinated way. Specific specialisation courses may be organised within LEAs, but are sometimes also offered by professional groups (e.g. National Council for Special Education and National Association for Remedial Education). Various organisations also offer courses. For example, the Spastics Society runs a centre (Castle Priory College) specifically intended to provide short courses. Individual Colleges and Universities also offer short courses, and the DES has its series of Regional Courses.

It is evident that, as LEAs formulate more articulated policies for the development of service delivery, specific requirements for short courses will emerge. For example, those LEAs which plan to extend the consultancy and support roles of special school staff, will clearly be needing to provide the staff concerned with the requisite skills which their previous roles and functions may not have demanded. Subject specialists in ordinary schools will, as has already been mentioned, need to have appropriate curricular extension components added to their courses. Similarly, management courses for heads and other senior staff will require 'special needs' components of relevance to their developing responsibilities.

Conclusion

In-service education for teachers of children with special educational needs can be seen to require a broad spectrum of course provision. The present surge in demand for these aspects of service delivery, coinciding as it does with constraints on resources, makes it clear that overall policies need to be developed to ensure the best application of those resources which do exist. At the same time, it is important that the education service is not seen in isolation from other services, both statutory and voluntary, in the development of service delivery. This point applies equally to in-service education. The Warnock Report already advocated cross-discipline in-service education, but little provision has yet been made for courses along these lines.

The whole area of in-service education for special needs teaching provides a challenge for those involved, to free themselves from the organisational assumptions which currently seem to limit the development of courses. At the same time, there is a corresponding responsibility that new approaches to in-service education should be adequately evaluated, so that development can be firmly grounded on evidence that the ultimate criteria of meeting children's special needs are met, in a form which does not result in impractical and unrealistic demands on teachers.

Chapter Eight

SPECIAL EDUCATION NEEDS POST-SCHOOL: TEACHER TRAINING
IMPLICATIONS

Nanette Whitbread

The main problems of equipping teachers in the post-compulsory
phases of education to cater for all those with special
educational needs in the Warnock definition and within the
context of the 1981 Education Act may be summarised as:

1. their lack of experience in teaching such students
because these have tended not to present themselves for any
forms of continued post-compulsory education in the past;

2. that a majority of further and adult education
teachers have not been trained to teach and that consequently
any in-service training must be directed at two disparate
groups, namely, those who have and those who have not undergone basic initial training;

3. the urgency of the task as the new clientele of
students, including many with evident special needs, is
presenting for new forms of further education and training
much of which is under the auspices of the Manpower Services
Commission.

Those whose special educational needs have been unrecog-
nised, unmet or unsatisfactorily met during their years
of compulsory schooling have been sufficiently disenchanted
with education to have been unlikely to present themselves
for further education beyond sixteen either in school or
in a college of further education, though some later gain
the self-knowledge and courage to seek help through the
informal network of adult and community education. Projects
mounted or supported by the Adult Literacy and Basic Skills
Unit may then come to their aid: much of the expertise and
resources of ALBSU are focused on ad hoc staff development
and support for largely untrained, and often volunteer,
tutors who are attempting to meet the previously neglected
special educational needs of adults. The number of such
adults is considerable - variously estimated at a constant

2-4 million in terms of functional illiteracy alone - and an indictment of the education service. There must be many further millions who are functioning at well below their potential in various aspects of their adult life, only a few of whom become sufficiently self-motivated to enrol on the small number of not widely accessible special 'access' or 'bridging' courses to equip them for regular courses in further or higher education.

So the background to the present problem is that by effectively rejecting and neglecting many of those with special educational needs once it no longer has to contain and attempt or pretend to cater for them, the mainstream education service has hitherto had little experience of diagnosing and meeting special needs beyond sixteen. (Those earlier identified as needing special provision outside mainstream schooling may have been able to go on to similar special provision, but these fall into rather specific categories.)

Post-compulsory education being by definition voluntary, there has been an implicit - sometimes even explicit - assumption that it was for students to fit the courses: those who don't fit may perhaps be helped to find another that fits, or else quit. This is undoubtedly an overly harsh judgement on the many FE lecturers who try very hard to meet their students' individual needs, coax and coach them, and on the increasing number of colleges that have set up counselling services to provide something akin to the pastoral role of schools, as well as on the LEAs and Regional Advisory Councils that publicise which colleges make certain kinds of special educational provision or have facilities to accommodate wheelchaired students and so on. These are humane responses, many of which pre-date the Warnock Report. The function of traditional FE has been to provide externally designed courses in vocational education and training to equip for skilled employment those who present themselves or are sent by their employers. Moreover, the predominantly part-time model of vocational education and training puts a high premium on self-motivation, commitment and ability to cope, while also making difficult much indivi- dualised follow-up additional provision. This explains the lack of experience within further education in identifying and meeting special needs.

However, through the evolution of 'second chance' academic further education through GCE over the past thirty years, the FE service has been responsive in enabling late developers and those who, for various reasons, failed to achieve adequately at school to do so later. Again, this has been largely a response to those who find their own motivation and present themselves for full-time or part-time courses. Thus FE can be a partial safety net for some victims of earlier non-selection for academic secondary schooling, provided they have the confidence to present themselves. More recently, special access courses have been developed in some colleges in collaboration with institutions of higher education, precisely to attract and serve those who have suffered educational disadvantage but now wish to be helped to remedy the situation. Such courses are an extension of the 'second chance' principle with particular reference to ethnic minority students, and are self-contained ventures.

The mainstream FE system has not hitherto *required* FE teachers to be particularly attuned to students' possible special educational needs. Those in greatest need of such help have generally not appeared in FE classes, just as they have not stayed on at school. The arrival first of YOPS and now YTS, the pioneering of pre-vocational courses by the vocational examining bodies and the initiative of the Further Education Curriculum Review and Development Unit (FEU) on *A Basis for Choice* and now the Secretary of State's conversion to a Certificate of Pre-Vocational Education at 17+ have significantly changed the FE world. These developments, rather than the 1981 Education Act, have had a major impact on post-compulsory education, creating the 'new FE' in parallel with the 'new Sixth'. Recognising, identifying, diagnosing and providing for youngsters with persistent or passing special educational needs beyond sixteen becomes an educational imperative.

It is an imperative with which FE teachers are grappling pragmatically as they design new courses for a new clientele whose educational needs they have not previously encountered to any great extent. They are tackling these tasks not only without the light of much previous relevant experience but also largely without benefit of previous pedagogic training themselves. The limited progress made in the nine years since the first Haycocks Report found that some two-thirds of the FE teaching force was untrained in teaching has left this substantial residual problem. Extensive and intensive staff development of both trained and untrained, full-time and part-time further education teachers is now a consequential imperative of considerable urgency.

The FEU was quick to recognise and accept the challenge of Warnock, publishing a Response to the White Paper in the autumn of 1980, a review of current and completed research relating to young people in the 14-19 age range with special educational needs a year later, and by the end of 1982 proposals for a curriculum framework for young people in further education with moderate learning difficulties entitled *Skills for Living*. Such publications and the efforts of FEU field officers provide essential support for in-college staff development, and follow on the initiatives taken by the Centre for Educational Disadvantage when that was closed down as an unwarranted quango.

It is recognised that specific INSET must build on the basic foundations of ITT in developing understanding of and provision for special educational needs among teachers in the primary and secondary phases, but in-service staff development in further and adult phases cannot assume such a continuum. Moreover, much of the curriculum development and consequential or parallel staff development for the 'new FE' is by implication concerned with new educational needs particular to the new student clientele, as evidenced by the new jargon of 'social and life skills' and 'experimental learning'. Indeed, teachers of the 'new Sixth' are finding that FEU publications are not irrelevant for their new tasks. Untrained graduate school teachers are probably concentrated in traditional academic sixth-form GCE classes, to judge from their distribution in types of school, so that teachers of the 'new Sixth' are likely to be drawn from the trained force with a pedagogic background from which to approach their new tasks. Staff development through INSET will be necessary if they are to meet the continuing special educational needs of those who choose to stay on at school beyond sixteen.

If the tertiary, post-compulsory phase is to match the various special needs of those youngsters it has hitherto largely neglected it must do so across both schools and further education. There must therefore be INSET and staff development, backed by research much of which will appropriately be action research and pragmatic. INSET must, however, target different groups of teachers in terms of their prior knowledge and experience: an urgent target group must surely be untrained.

If the YTS is to serve the youngsters and not just employers (and the government's political need to massage them from the unemployment statistics) their special needs must also be identified and provided for. But the private agencies so favoured by the MSC are unlikely to be able to do this. Referral to further education might be a possibility, but it seems more likely that these private agencies will selectively reject youngsters they perceive as deviant or as posing problems, leaving them for the colleges to pick up. If the proposals in the White Paper, *Training for Jobs,* are implemented the prospect of effective provision for youngsters with special needs on work-related courses will be minimal, as the courses and staffing requirements will not be quality controlled by the education service.

The task of equipping for an enlightened post-Warnock approach to matching the educational and training needs of *all* young people over sixteen, with their diverse and sometimes complex special needs, is immense and has hardly begun to be tackled. The FEU's 1981 review of research showed the further education service still perceiving special needs and provision largely in terms of those relating to physical handicap or to learning failure for which an impoverished basic skills curriculum was an appropriate response. Haycock's model in-post initial training for further education teachers will have to pay far more attention to developing awareness and sensitivity for recognising special needs in parallel with INSET and research for building specialist expertise and knowledge concerning the 16-19 age range. Historic barriers between schools and FE have to be broken down in respect of attitudes, perceptions and even vocabulary of sectoral jargon - and this must surely involve joint post-experience INSET. This would necessitate unpicking certain administrative patterns of sectorally allocated finance within LEA and DES bureaucracies. Perhaps a start might be made with a focus on CPVE.

Chapter Nine

A FRENCH PERSPECTIVE ON SPECIAL NEEDS

Dominique Paty

This is a review of French schooling arrangements for those pupils who in Great Britain would be said to manifest 'special needs' in education. Our scrutiny is confined to the years of adolescence, the last years of compulsory education, eleven to sixteen. Any significant differences of structure in elementary education will be highlighted if they affect our topic.

The French Background

Especially since the early 1970s, there has been a tendency towards quite considerable integration of pupils with 'special needs' in the ordinary system, even if specific support is provided for them (whether or not by the 'special education' sector of the education service). This development is seen especially in the increasing involvement of the Ministry of Education, although as we shall see the Ministries of Health and Social Services continue to play a role.

First, a list of the main structures, starting with those for the most severely handicapped, and moving to systems for children 'without problems'. We will refer later to particular cases which may be smaller in number but illuminating: agricultural schools, employer-based training schools, and some which are established for distinct social categories.

Pupils with severe or substantial mental deficiencies are attached to specialised institutions under the wing of the Ministry of Health, or under joint administration of the health and education ministries. Those with severe motor or sensory handicaps are educated either in institutions directed by the Ministry of Health (especially blind and deaf children) or in specialised establishments under the Ministry of Education. With the exception of these two types of establishment, arrangements are made within the ordinary national education system. Within the framework of the secondary school, there are special education sections for young people with moderate intellectual deficiency, and there are also some specialised classes for pupils with one or other type of handicap.

Beyond all these young people who have been identified by a 'Commission' (see below) as having handicaps (physical, mental or behavioural), there are a large number of pupils who could be described as having 'special needs' in education, if the term is extended somewhat, and who are in the ordinary system, whether or not grouped together in remedial classes.

Some Issues and Problems

Looking at this variety of situations, one could ask who defines the 'special need' or its French equivalent, who poses the questions, who responds, and who evaluates? One important point is pupil-mobility and institutional flexibility, or in contrast, the way handicap may be made permanent by institutionalisation, in structures which are self-feeding.

Placement in our category of establishments (medical institutions for education, learning or vocational training) is proposed by the Special Education Commission of each local authority. These institutions take pupils who have a substantial handicap, especially of a mental category, to such an extent that one could wonder whether the notion of 'special need' is not in essence a need to exclude on the part of the social environment. Teachers sometimes find it difficult to have these pupils accepted in, for example, sports teams and associations open to the public.

This raises two major questions, which are not strictly speaking educational. Handicap in young people often has a strong social component. In the years preceding elementary education, nursery schools introduce children aged two to six to schooling, but in France nursery education is not compulsory. Current policy for social services is to retain these children in their family settings for as long as possible, if need be with the support of psychological or child guidance services, but with no compensation for weaknesses in 'pre-school' introductions to education. In the nursery schools, some attempt is now made to diagnose and prevent handicap. But for children who have had no school experience below the age of six, admission to elementary school is a formidable moment for handicap to be exposed. If the handicap is not too severe, the child does have the benefit of some educational and psychological support while attending elementary school (especially through child guidance centres). But for a significant number of pupils, therapy and social support comes too late. So there is no close

connection between school work and special education until a
child is moved to a specialised institution, from which there
is little prospect of returning to a normal programme.

The second problem is located further on, at the level of
employment. The laws on recruiting handicapped people to
places of work are inadequately applied. 'Work Aid Centres',
public centres which employ handicapped adults, do not cover
the whole range of needs, either in quantity or in quality.
The current economic crisis is shifting the demand for
qualifications to the lowest levels. Jobs which could
previously be found by those with moderate mental deficiencies
are now frequently filled by people who have completed a
normal education, or even those with advanced qualifications.

So the tasks of the medical institutions (educational or
vocational) are difficult to define at present, for want of a
sense of direction. There is a noticeably brutal break
between the period of schooling (in whatever setting, with
whatever range of learning activities and individual attention) and 'the start in working life'. But there would be
doubtless insoluble problems if there were any significant
extension beyond existing establishments. For former pupils
of the medical institutes may well merge into the mass of
job-hunters from schools, but are difficult to connect to the
significant numbers of young people already on training
schemes. These training schemes, which already have weaknesses for pupils coming from the 'ordinary' system of
schooling, hardly seem appropriate for young handicapped
people.

To begin to ask such questions, it is certain that
the number of pupils who return to the ordinary channels is
too low. As we have seen, this is largely due to the
structure of employment. But it is also true that the medical
institutes, whether educational or vocational, are highly
autonomous structures, and indeed inward-looking. Their means
of financing make them relatively dependent on the client
source. So one has to ask whether these institutes will be
able to take the initiative of their own volition to try
systematically to feed back into the ordinary schools those
pupils with whom they are achieving good results.

For adolescents with motor handicaps, whether physical or
sensory, there is a choice of specialised establishments:
schools offering general education, or remedial schools
offering general and vocational training. There may also be
classes for the handicapped in ordinary schools, or individual
pupils may be integrated in ordinary classes. These last two
solutions, where they are possible, are of course the ones

which authorities are trying to develop, even if they demand classes of reduced size.

The special education sections (SES) are incorporated in secondary schools, but within these they have the benefit of their own structure, of specialist staff, and of additional resources. In principle, they are intended for pupils with moderate deficiencies, but in practice they also take in under-achievers, whatever the cause of their failure. They are thought to achieve quite good results, due partly to highly individualised teaching. The technical training offered there is coupled with teachers' involvement in the employer/pupil relationship during work experience courses; and there is often some follow-up after young people have left the education system. For some years, attempts have been made to remove the barriers between special education sections and the rest of the establishment. There is also some question of them being extended beyond the age of sixteen and leading to elements of vocational certification. For the moment, the resources of these attached units seem somewhat under-used. Parents are sometimes loath to have their children admitted to these sections, for fear of them being labelled as inferior. Indeed, even when they are pupils within the whole school, we have seen that there is insufficient permeability between these sections and the rest of the establishment. Often, teachers in the school and those in the special education section hardly know each other and have no appreciation of each other's work.

The basic problem remains that of placement in special education sections, often deflected from their original purpose of taking in those with mild deficiencies. If pupils are taken in who have not been able to adapt elsewhere, it is the institution which has a 'special need' and not the pupil.

School Failure

Finally, we must touch on a category which is numerically much more important (in proportions which vary from one school to another): pupils who have been regrouped for the last two years of secondary school in particular classes called basic pre-vocational classes. For example, in 1984-85, it is estimated that about 130,000 pupils were placed in these classes along with pre-apprenticeship classes, with 70,000 in special education sections for the last two years of school, compared with 1,500,000 in ordinary classes. These pre-vocational classes are intended for school failures. They are supposed to receive some general education, as well as pre-vocational training. All too often, the openings for pupils from these sections are problematical.

112

Attempts are now being made to cut down their numbers or at least to penetrate the dividing wall between them and 'normal' classes. But if these separate groups which too often look like blind alleys were to disappear, then some other form of separate grouping for pupils in great difficulty would be created. Indeed, for more than twenty years, there has been a succession of such structures. They spring from initial hopes (reduced numbers of pupils, dedicated and motivated teaching, more active and up-to-date teaching methods) but are then discovered to be unable to reintroduce their pupils to the mainstream. As soon as they are seen as 'refuse tips', they are even more devalued, in the eyes of pupils, teachers, and parents.

In fact, it is evident that this is a question of the structural needs of the education system itself, which has not yet managed to set itself objectives which it can achieve. Without wishing to categorise these pupils as having 'special needs', other than the need of some additional teaching support, and so without excluding them, the system keeps them in its bosom, though uncomfortably on one side.

It should be noted that within the main national system of education, there are examples of individualised responses to pupils' temporary needs. Re-education (speech therapy, psycho-motor skills, etc.) it is true is more frequent and better organised for primary education where it is parents' occupations which determine the structure: the children of boatpeople are offered residential schooling for their necessarily intermittent education. For gipsy children, nothing better has been found that a few primary school teachers to follow them in 'bus-schools', without any provision for secondary education.

Conclusion

Some general conclusions are possible. There is a range of responses, which in principle is broad and diversified. But specialised structures in fact take in a less 'handicapped' population than intended; that is to say, they also serve as a means of exclusion and withdrawal for pupils with problems of behaviour and adjustment. Moreover, they often operate too rigidly and separately, which of course reinforces their role as a means of exclusion. So the work of teachers in these contexts is doubtless not as useful as it could be.

This tendency to shift each category of pupils towards a system not intended for them indicates that there is a more general problem. Poor school organisation, unadapted curriculum content and inappropriate methods can sometimes create problems which are beyond the control of teachers.

In France, we speak of 'failure at school' rather than of 'special needs', a notion which I find woolly and ambiguous, since it refers to the personality of a pupil. It has to be admitted that the notion of 'failure at school', even though it states the situation, has pejorative connotations, with the sense of permanence in failure (and indeed, statistics show that pupils who make a poor start to their first year of primary schooling have constant difficulties subsequently). However that may be, 'palliative' or 'remedial' measures have not as yet been far-reaching. If our famous 'failure at school' is to be forestalled, then the models offered implicitly or explicitly to pupils and assimilated by teachers have to be modified. This does not exclude the possibility of defining (but rigorously and with a precise educational response) those cases where it is necessary to talk of a pupil's 'handicap'.

The success stories are interesting. Sensory handicaps appear to have found a kind of adapted schooling within ordinary establishments: perhaps because there are specialist teachers trained deliberately alongside other teachers? Moreover, the agricultural schools have developed their courses more closely to the cultural models which are relevant to their pupils: and doubtless there is a good example for others. The special education sections have worked very well in certain cases, managing to introduce to the world of work young people who demonstrated very obvious 'special needs'; but these cases have always been in sections which have not been deflected from their precise brief.

If these special education sections have on the whole been resistant to the various 'deflections' mentioned above, and have resisted them more successfully than other comparable systems, this may well be due to the training of their teachers. They are former teachers of 'normal' classes, who for the most part have undergone further special training conferring diploma qualifications and financial promotion. This endows them with a specific professional identity in relation to their colleagues, and with a certain institutional power, which perhaps reinforces their tendency towards segregation.

In the case of contributors who have been trained initially straight into special education without experience of ordinary teaching, there is often a noticeably reactive attitude towards the educational and social systems, which can lead to ambiguous positions of identifying with pupils as 'victims' of those 'bad' teachers. On the other hand, those teachers drawn from the ordinary system who work voluntarily in the basic pre-vocational classes and who acquire a certain amount of training on the job (for example as a result of pedagogical reforms), are at a disadvantage inside school establishments, even if they are achieving comparable results.

As for the content of teacher-training, it would seem to be particularly important to move towards some common basis. Highly specialised teachers may not be aware of or may have forgotten the problems encountered in general teaching. Teachers in ordinary classes do not know what is done with pupils with whom they have failed. This hardly improves the prospect for team dialogue or mobility across structures! Certain disciplines should be introduced or developed in all forms of training: social sciences and psychology. In professional studies, there needs to be more thorough and more widely based research into different ways of studying in depth, and that requires genuine inter-disciplinary work, which is always difficult. But after all, is not one of the considerations a shared analysis of different educative practices?

My own experience as a teacher-trainer in this context has shown me the sheer weight and complexity of resistance to that need, however frequently it may be invoked as a ritual. We all respond to pupils who pose problems, but we do not easily unveil the nature of our response, whether or not it is fruitful, or of our own needs. So we often deprive ourselves of the very basis of professional development which we need in this context, and which still remains to be defined.

Chapter Ten

INITIAL TEACHER EDUCATION AND THE ROLE OF THE SUPPORT AGENCIES

John Quicke

The ACSET report on 'Teaching Training and Special Educational Needs' acknowledges that the awareness of special educational needs will have to permeate the work of all tutors and thus clearly emphasises that SEN should not be treated as a marginal component but as an integral part of mainstream 'curriculum and method' on initial training courses. It suggests that such courses, even if they last only one year, should encourage an awareness of the nature of special needs; of the appropriate teaching methods and materials across the curriculum to meet the needs of individual pupils; the need to collaborate with parents; and familiarity with the range of specialist services available to pupils and parents. Since most existing staff employed in initial teacher training (ITT) will probably not have the necessary expertise, the report recommends that tutors in training institutions should follow appropriate staff development programmes.

In this chapter I shall begin with some general comments on the ACSET proposals before going on to discuss special needs 'awareness' courses in initial teacher training and the place on these of an introduction to the roles of support agencies. In the last part I shall comment more specifically on the nature of collaboration between the teacher and the support agencies and the perspective on this which is relevant for ITT.

Teacher Education or Teaching Training?

Most of us on reflection would agree that teacher training is something of a misnomer and what we really mean is teacher education. There are some profound philosophical principles at stake here which are of more than just academic interest, witness the 'blurring' to which the Manpower Services Commission refers in many of its handouts. All the more reason, then, why we should be a bit touchy on the point and insist that we are mainly at the education rather than training end of things. It is for this reason I find the statement in the ACSET document that tutors in ITT may need training as much as their students patronising and anti-educational in the extreme, both in relation to the staff concerned and the students. It seems to represent the worst starting point possible for policies of collaboration between colleagues with historically different roles, functions and experiences. There is more than a faint echo here of the deficit model so long the butt of criticism amongst progressive and radicals and yet here used in all its inglorious fallaciousness to impugn the subject tutors.

Surely a better approach would be one that began with an open discussion involving all tutors where views on the assumptions and practices of special education could be given a thorough airing and a rough assessment made of how this topic was currently being dealt with on the course. During the course of such discussion one would anticipate the emergence of some familiar tension points - a commitment to mixed ability teaching yet a concern that academic standards should not be affected; a misconception of the scope of special education and of the role and function of support agencies; the contradiction generated by the artificial split between subject and child centred teaching, between the 'welfare' and the academic curriculum and between 'special' and 'ordinary'; a blindness to the political and philosophical beliefs underpinning the practice of special education; the assumption that special educators have privileged knowledge about learning and behavioural difficulties.

What is required to get movement in the system is a recognition of the social, historical and 'territorial' construction of most of these tension points so that the ground can be cleared for genuine collaboration based on a common interest. It seems to me that one does not have to look very far for a concern which typically preoccupies all tutors whatever their specialities. What I have in mind is encapsulated in this statement taken from a report which was itself a product of collaboration across professional divides 'Yet we believe that the problems of under achievement . . . and of disaffection will be resolved effectively only when careful attention is paid to issues of coherence and balance in the curriculum' (Hargreaves, 1984, para 3.4.11).

These issues are raised by the authors in the context of a discussion of the action of whole curriculum planning, which is regarded by them as an important aspect of the way forward in comprehensive education and one which inevitably involves cooperation between individual teachers and coordination of departments. Whole curriculum planning is something to which all teachers can make a contribution, and for which all of them should be prepared in initial teacher education. From such a starting point all the issues about the nature and practice of special education will automatically be raised; and since an intergrationist philosophy and a concern to provide education suited to the interests, experiences, abilities and backgrounds of all children are clearly an essential part of whole curriculum strategies, there may be no need to refer explicitly to children as having special educational needs as such. Curriculum and method courses should be grounded in the notion that all children are special.

Awareness Courses in Special Educational Needs

If the above strategy is successful what is the point of having an 'awareness course' at all? It could be argued that such a course would inevitably introduce a segregationist element into a programme aimed at facilitating an engagement with the principles and practices of the comprehensive school movement. However, in the current period, we are not at this point, and it seems to me that there is still a need to provide students with an overview of contemporary issues in special education, provided this is done carefully in a way which is not counterproductive.

The content of such a course requires much more thought than we have previously given it. Hidden and overt messages reinforcing the separateness of special education were typical of much of what went on before. Awareness courses that begin with an emphasis on the alleged characteristics of children with special needs, with discovery and identification, are clearly suspect because they easily lead to an historical, reified view of special needs which is precisely what we want to avoid. Far better to start with an explanation of why a concept of special educational needs was thought to be necessary, how ideas about this were legitimated by 'expert knowledge' and what alternative perspectives are in play in the current period.

After this basically historical introduction, issues could be dealt with in a way which dovetailed with either awareness courses that the students were pursuing, in accordance with the principles of whole curriculum planning. I am thinking in particular of components on multi-professional relationships; the common curriculum; home-school liaison; teacher expectation; equal opportunities which one would anticipate being included as essential topics in the

education/professional curriculum of a modern course.
Thus, on the special needs course, discussion of the notions
of special curricula, or curricula for slow learners
or modified curricula *a la* Form 7 could be related to the
debate about the common curriculum. Home-school liaison would
provide a context for the parents-as-partners perspective;
teacher expectation would be linked with a thorough examination of labelling, stigma and deviant careers in relation to
children officially defined as having special educational
needs; and unequal opportunities due to gender, ethnicity and
social class with a discussion of why certain groups
were disproportionately represented in special education.

Intra professional collaboration would be a theme endemic
to the course as a whole and in relation to special needs it
would probably take the form of exploring new types of
relationships with remedial teacher and discussing possible
roles for designated and resource teachers in the ordinary
school. The theme of multi-professional relationships will
relate to an introduction to the work of the external
specialists or, as I prefer to call them, the support agencies
and it is to a consideration of this particular topic I now
turn. It is self evident from the foregoing that we
would seek to sensitise students to the need for collaborative
relationships with the support agencies but before elaborating
on this I think it is important to have a closer look
at the meaning of the term collaboration.

The Meaning of Collaboration

Teachers collaborating because of a common interest in whole
curriculum planning and comprehensive education is one
thing; teachers collaborating with other professionals about
children with special needs is quite another. The inter-
professional divide is a more difficult one to cross because
a common occupational culture and thus shared meanings cannot
be assumed.

It is for this reason that I interrupt the flow of the
discussion to go back over ground which has been only lightly
touched upon up until this point. So far, I hope the reader
has been able to share my optimism as to the future success of
strategies aimed at realising a system of cooperation amongst
teachers. Yet perhaps this optimism may be construed as
rather heady and a touch naive in view of the dismal track
record of previous attempts to create such a system and so I
want to proceed more cautiously.

A teacher to whom I was talking recently about collaborative learning remarked upon her uneasiness about the term

120

which for her evoked images of French women having their heads shaved because they had collaborated with the Nazis. This connotation is unfortunate but it does raise one or two obvious but often forgotten points. In a situation where cooperation with a member of another profession is suggested as an appropriate course of action, we must ask in the first instance whether either or both the parties concerned were in any sense constrained to collaborate and, second, even if they both collaborated voluntarily, would it in any case necessarily be a 'good thing'?

The first question reminds one of the double think involved when a top-down change process is being sold as something which is 'self-directed'. This form of self-deception is typical of many psychological approaches to change which takes various forms but have in common a naivety about social and political realities (see Quicke, 1978). Teachers are rarely openly forced to submit to the collaborative mode (despite stories of them being lined up in Indian file at cross-curricular course registration centres by over enthusiastic local authority advisers!) but there may nevertheless be considerable informal pressure on them to do so, and this not from their equals in a democratic set up but from colleagues who have the power to influence their career development. When power is distributed unequally one tends to be sceptical about teachers freely choosing to collaborate.

In schools one suspects that, infra dig though it may be to pull rank, when negotiations are going badly there is always the danger that teachers with more power and status will attempt to impose their will on those with less. Such is the inevitability of this occurrence, in my view, that one can never hope to achieve genuine voluntary participation in collaborative enterprises unless hierarchical structures amongst school staffs are demolished and teacher/teacher relationships are democratised.

A similar point can be made about teachers' relationships with support services. Here it is not so much power to affect career chances which is significant, so much as power to determine how a child's identity will be constructed and the consequences which follow from this. It is important to bear in mind that relative to some of the support agencies, e.g. educational psychologists and, in particular, doctors, teachers have a lowly status and this may mean that in the multi-professional team, their views will not be equally valued.

The second question referred to above probes the notion that collaboration is inherently a positive concept, i.e. an

121

idea which derives from a view of human beings which assumes that maximising social interaction will usually result in individual defences being pulled down and that this will usually bring out the best in people. Now, although we can accept the truth of this in social relationships bounded by a common notion of 'good', it is certainly not universally and necessarily true. Even within education where we would expect some agreement over ends, if not means, there are many circumstances where collaboration is not possible because of fundamental value differences between the parties concerned. I think it is important for teachers and students to be aware of their right to choose in this matter. To collaborate or to establish some other form of *modus operandi* is a rational decision based on what we estimate as the degree of give and take possible in relation to particular persons or groups, and our assessment of the social values and beliefs which are being propagated on the other side of the professional barrier.

The Support Agencies

These considerations should provide us with guide lines on how to deal with the role of support agencies on an awareness course. Support itself is a difficult term which may require some clarification. In schools it is often used to refer to those systems which allow the academic or instructional system to function smoothly and have the purpose of propping up existing curricula and organisation. In this sense it has connotations of being a status quo maintaining and conservative force. However, it is possible to use the term in a collaborative context so that what one really means is not one way propping up but 'mutual support'. Another confusion may arise from the therapeutic meaning of the term when it is associated with activities of professionals in relation to their clients. Thus one refers to social workers or psychiatrists supporting families or educational psychologists supporting teachers. The same point applies here as to support systems - the question who is supporting whom must be taken seriously and is answered with the notion that genuine teamwork implies mutual, not one way, support. As the following discussion will demonstrate, it is as valid to look upon an 'external specialist' as being supported by a teacher as it is to conceive of the latter as supported by the specialist.

One practical point to consider is how much time should be devoted to the discussion of the role of support agencies on an initial education course. Most teachers do not have extensive contracts with such agencies and it is probably the case that inexperienced teachers have even less.

However, there is no doubt that many support agencies themselves would like to have a close liaison with teachers and perceive a dialogue with them as an important part of their preventive role, even if they have often mistakenly considered this as consultancy rather than collaborative work. Similarly, there are changes in the way teachers are beginning to use external professionals, despite the influence of the backward looking 'end of the line' model such as that recommended by the Warnock Committee in its outline referral procedures. In any case, it is up to tutors to encourage students to view the agencies in a way which differs from the traditional image of the 'visiting expert' and to use them as a community resource which the pupils in their charge have a right to expect to be deployed wisely for them. The perceptions picked up in initial education will inevitably influence attitudes at the start of teaching careers and these are at risk of becoming permanently narrow and restricted in the absence of any countervailing tendencies.

In general, the most important message to get across to students is that what they should expect is more than just an exchange of views or information but a dialogue with the support agency in which various possibilities for meeting needs can be explored in a manner which is not bounded by professional rituals and is open, honest and creative. If such relationships do not pertain then questions should be asked about what is causing the blockage in the system. By asking questions, stating their expectations and making demands on behalf of their pupils, teachers are in a position to influence the way support agencies develop their roles as well as themselves being open to influence from the latter.

Which support agencies should be dealt with is another important question. There are up to thirty or so who might be involved with children with special needs and they clearly cannot all be discussed in great depth. If one has to suggest priorities I would have thought that the most likely candidates for the top of the list would be those professionals who are essentially education-based and typically referred to in relation to learning and behaviour difficulties, including truancy and school refusal. However, workers in social and medical services should certainly not be excluded.

The Education Welfare Officer

Collaboration with parents has already been mentioned as a key area and the professionals of the support agencies can be of great assistance here. In particular, one might single out the Education Welfare Officer as a key figure. Bearing in mind the above discussion, students should be encouraged to develop a perspective of what they think the EWO's role should be. I think it is possible for them at least to begin thinking about it even though they will not have time to familiarise themselves with all the alternatives for this group. Similarly, they should expect EWOs to be making certain demands on them. Generally, one would anticipate them construing the role as one where the EWO had a preventive as well as crisis function, representing an important link between teachers and homes and facilitated contact with parents. They might also consider ways in which the EWO could contribute to the counselling and pastoral work of the school and may actively encourage the development of this aspect of their role. On the other hand, with reference to the point made above on collaboration, they should not feel obliged to cooperate with an EWO who construes the role in a way which does not complement what they are trying to do in the classroom. One would imagine that they would be opposed to an EWO working in a more traditional manner as a 'kid catcher' rather than a social worker or as an ambulance service when things go wrong.

The Educational Psychologist

Another key figure is the educational psychologist. Collaboration with EPs may prove to be difficult if there is too much distance between educational aims and objectives. Thus a visiting EP may, for instance, insist on defining a problem in terms of learning difficulties 'possessed' by the child or in terms of what the EP perceives as the teacher's personal 'deficits' but which from the teacher's viewpoint are more to do with the constraints in that particular school. A very traditional EP may be primarily concerned, in most contacts with the school, with special placement decisions. In which case, the teacher should demand to be involved in all such decisions and insist on face to face dialogue with the EP. On the other hand, it might be possible for a teacher to reinforce the role of the EP when it is clearly changing in a direction which is compatible with the teacher's philosophy. The hope would be that the EP would construe the role as one where there was less emphasis on 'assessment and disposal' of children with special educational needs and more concern for prevention, and advice and support in the ordinary classroom setting. The class teacher should anticipate - and this would have to be negotiated with teacher colleagues - the right to have direct access to the EP and not to have to go through a bureaucratic layer in order for them to discuss children. Teachers should expect to be invited to join multi-professional teams and will hope that the EP is prepared to share knowledge with them and be capable of discussing all manner of educational issues - the educational needs of particular children, the 'hidden curriculum', the curriculum itself, and classroom organisation.

I feel that this approach of encouraging students to contemplate how they might actively engage in reconstructing their own and others' professional practice has the potential to generate much needed change in the system. However, impediments to the developments of more democratic open and non-directive relationships are not to be underestimated. Potential barriers have been hinted at in the foregoing discussion of the changing role of the EWO and EP, but these are nothing compared with those that need to be overcome when one considers relationships with professions which are not under the educational umbrella but which have an historical association with the education, health and welfare of children with special needs. I am thinking in particular of professionals in the medical services.

Medical Services

Whilst students coming on the course will probably have only a vague impression of the work of EWOs and EPs, most of them will have some knowledge of the role and function of the medical profession. No doubt they will have been just as susceptible as all of us to the acquisition of common stereotypes of the 'good doctor' and may also have adopted a deferential attitude towards this high status profession. Possibly also they will not understand the limitations of medical knowledge and imagine that doctors know more about the educational aspects of dealing with 'disabilities' than they actually do. It is important, therefore, that when discussing pupils' special educational needs we look at the medical contribution sympathetically but critically in a way that does not automatically reinforce its classical embrace. Such reinforcement is easy, particularly when most of the language we use continues to signal that there is a medical expert out there who knows all about these things and is a specialist to whom the teacher should defer. Diagnosis, treatment, cerebral palsy, hyperactivity, dyslexia, disorder, handicaps, therapy, syndrome, and dysphasia are all terms which carry with them the implication that medical responsibility is primary. Using them in a mystifying way can disable the teacher as easily as it can the parent.

Moreover, introducing the medical profession and its terminology in a merely information giving manner may have ideological consequences which go beyond the relatively small group of children with special needs for whom medical explanations do have direct implications for teaching. Striking images of children with gross physical handicaps can exert a lasting influence on how special needs are perceived, and are strongly suggestive of a marginal rather than a broad concept of special needs, putting individual deficit rather than curriculum and organisation almost literally at the heart of things. The dangers here are such that serious considera- tion should be given to whether medical support services should be discussed at all on initial education courses. If the main emphasis is on learning and behaviour difficulties there is clearly no need for extensive coverage of the medical input. However, I think the omission would be a mistake because there would be no opportunity for students to examine critically their own assumptions about medicine, and as they would be unable to develop a basis on which to con- struct their own views about community and educational medicine. The context is important. Whilst special needs awareness courses seem an obvious slot for this topic, it should not be forgotten that the role of medicine in education is much broader than terms like 'handicap' and 'disability' would suggest and that medical matters could be incorporated into the curriculum in a variety of ways, e.g. via health education.

None of this is to suggest that medically based profes- sions provide no examples of good practice in the special needs area. For instance, some physiotherapists have under- stood the need not to retain too tight a grip on their exper- tise and the importance of disseminating their skills and knowledge amongst teachers. They have recognised the importance of delivering physiotherapy in a way which causes the minimum of disruption to 'normal' educational processes for the child concerned and of being open to suggestions from teachers. Similarly, some health visitors have regarded it as an important aspect of their role that they make a contri- bution to health education in schools.

The Social Worker

In addition to medical services, the other important non- education based support agency to consider is the social worker. Again, the same points need to be borne in mind as when considering collaborative relations with other profes- sionals, although there is clearly less of a status gap between teacher and social worker than between teacher and doctor. Collaboration will be difficult if social workers, say, are so preoccupied with family pathology that they tend to look at all families in a distorted mirror or prefer explanations of behaviour which are always family centred and seem to give the teacher no role to play. But many social workers have considerable experience of how young people view the problems that society thrusts upon them and how to relate to disaffected youth in a non-patronising and humanistic way which enables them to retrieve some of the dignity which school often denies them. Of course, the social worker should recognise that since, next to the parent, the only other adult who may see the 'client' on a day to day basis is the teacher then the latter clearly has a contribution to make in any assessment of treatment that may be envisaged. When the young person is in custody, under observation and assessment, in care or in a community home, the social worker has a clear duty to keep in touch with the school and the teacher should be kept informed of what is happening and, where necessary, be asked to give a report on former or current school behaviour and progress. Had schools and teachers been more' involved in legal/care processes, then perhaps some of the more notorious examples of deviant labelling and consequent delinquent careers could have been avoided. Ordinary school would have been recognised as a place where a young person in trouble could have been 'placed'. It is also worth noting that many of the controversies relating to the treatment of young offenders are similar in kind to those with which we are concerned in special education - decarceration parallels desegregation; intermediate treatment is a similar idea to a non-punishment approach to behaviour problems in school; community service finds echoes in alternative curricula; and labelling, of course, is rife in both areas. The literature on juvenile delinquency provides a useful collection of insights into 'disruptive' behaviour both in and out of school.

Conclusion

In this chapter I have suggested that initial teacher education is just as valid a site as post experience courses to begin the process of reconstructing intra and inter professional roles and relationships. Collaborative teachers should aim for relationships characterised by teamwork and negotiation, but have to bear in mind that their own values and beliefs or ideal self interests may in a particular instance contradict the partnership approach. Teachers have to ask what they have in common with the support agencies. In a school where children with special needs are not treated as a marginal out-group we would expect to find efforts being made to realise the comprehensive ideal. We would expect to find a concern to make mixed-ability teaching work; a concern to make learning less individualist and competitive and more community-oriented and cooperative and a concern with whole curriculum planning to meet the educational needs of all children, whatever their abilities, backgrounds, interests and experiences. And collaborative teachers, therefore, would require of support agencies that they share the concern to evolve processes which help them to achieve these aims.

It is important to establish this point because there are clearly some circumstances when support agencies approach teachers with interests which are basically different, and it is essential for teachers to understand that they have a perfect right to confront and, if necessary, reject the expertise on offer. They may be strengthened in this resolve by being familiar with the critique of professionalism on which calls for deprofessionalisation and reprofessionalisation have been founded (see Wilding, P., 1982). For instance, they should not be mystified by claims of neutrality when it is self evident that social values and political beliefs are underpinning the support agencies' recommendations. In fact, as I have stressed in this chapter, teachers should not only question the neutrality pose but, if they feel there is a basis for negotiation, actively engage in changing the self-perception of the support agency concerned and thus its contribution to the task of making the education of children more genuinely comprehensive.

I do not think all these matters are too complex or controversial to deal with on initial education courses. Indeed, it would be irresponsible in my view to present support agencies as being above the politics of education and concerned only with providing a service of an impartial nature. Such an approach would send young teachers off on the wrong tack and could lay the foundations for cynicism, deference or defensiveness in their future inter-professional relationships.

Chapter Eleven

SUPPORT STRATEGIES FOR INSET FOCUSED ON SCHOOLS

Michael Jones

Over recent years, the pressure for change in secondary schools has increased and can be identified as acting on two main fronts:

i) The need to respond to an ever increasing spectrum of curriculum as reflected by the changes within our industrial society

and, in tension with the first,

ii) an increasing external evaluation vigilance from HMI to parents with an apparent decrease in resource provision.

The result is, on one side of the picture we have a large number of 'external' stimuli and initiatives; TVEI, the 1981 Act, increased focus on training provision and so on, whilst within schools the response will be, by and large, to tinker with what exists because the security of an institution and the practice of teachers does not normally induce a response that energetically and enthusiastically takes on board any degree of radical change.

The danger of imposing change is that it could lead to an entrenchment of attitudes rather than any elightened revision of practice. This danger is enhanced by demanding responses through externally imposed strategies, evaluation/inspection/LEA incursions, rather than positive support to encourage and enable a school to determine its own response. Such a response can only be sufficiently rapid or educationally worthwhile if the teachers within a school are genuinely involved in identifying need, which in turn can only occur if attitudes held by many teachers can be changed. There is sufficient evidence from schools that have become actively engaged in seeking responses to their own training needs, as opposed to a piecemeal response to what is offered externally, to be optimistic that with sensitive supporting strategies, changes in attitudes are possible.

Starting Points

We all respond positively to an involvement in the directing of our working lives. Effective teachers work towards inducing such involvement from children within their class-rooms. Within the structure of the school institution however, we seem to be going down a road that increasingly strips teachers of genuine responsibility for directing their own working environment. To bring about change in direction in which they operate, we need to examine and question the following:

a) Career Structures

The hallmark of the successful school must lie with the ability of teachers to perform the task of teaching. Currently, however, the tendency in many schools seems to encourage teachers to cast off the minutiae of daily management and not face real issues. Positions of responsi-bility are jealously guarded and an upward shifting of problems is therefore encouraged, as opposed to a downward movement of support to resolve problems at source. Rather than being a participant in planning, most teachers become receivers of messages, often confusing, sometimes conflicting, from above, leaving them to work in a partial vacuum of information. The current tendency of detailed job description allied to all scale posts does not improve the situation in that it becomes another message to teachers that they are not required to become involved in the full spectrum of their own work. Those on scale posts are encouraged, since they are being professionally tested in holding those positions, to exercise a hierarchical difference over their colleagues and to hold responsibility rather than share it with others. The cynical 'he's paid to do that' comment, even if not voiced, is present in attitude and results in an inevitable lowering of creative practice in schools.

The upward shift in daily management tasks has the other inevitable effect in that the senior staff in schools are busy maintaining the system of school, generally in a crisis management way, and are not spared the time, or the opportunity, to be leading their colleagues along a path of staff development that could begin to enable schools to really test their own professional achievements. A focus on career development based on an expectation of sharing experience and leading teams of teachers could do much to enhance the working environment for all teachers.

b) Conflicting Management Structures

Since the birth of the larger comprehensive schools, there appears to have been a largely unquestioned development of a dual management structure in schools, the Heads of House responsible for the 'pastoral' management of the school. The latter structure of course giving additional career opportunities for year heads, etc. Whereas it is easy to understand the career link with this development, the division is less easy to justify when the full education of the child is taken into account. When children are perceived to exist as two different and identifiable segments a resulting further dilution of teacher responsibility becomes obvious. The two management structures involved reach points of conflict and again, the full involvement of all teachers in the educational development of the children they teach is denied.

The effect on the children can rapidly become very negative in that it becomes the norm for teachers to refer onwards children with any level of difficulty, be it behavioural or a learning problem. Children can easily and unjustifiably be 'labelled' and many more learn quickly to 'play the system'. A built-in rejection system is established where problem of responsibility is passed on and the teacher's view of children becomes increasingly narrow. Whereas teachers *are* willing to take on the 'whole child', they are seldom given the opportunity to do so. The whole term 'special' educational needs adds to that rejection process, in that it assumes the existence of yet a further separate group of teachers who somehow are more able to deal with some parts of some children than others. The segmentation of schools and more significantly the education of children is thus further propagated.

The odd paradox that exists within teaching is the assumption that the teacher, particularly the 'specialist' teacher, is omnipotent within his/her classroom and yet, unless given a particular (and paid) brief to do so, is considered as not capable of contributing to decisions that effect the development of their own schools. There seems to be a built-in resistance to sharing, both of task and of management, that leads to a splintering effect rather than leading to a sense of cooperative identity. Yet within the classroom, group management and cooperative working is something all teachers aim for in order to provide the conditions through which much creative learning takes place. It should not be beyond the resource of any school to move towards a concept of teams of teachers focusing on the full spectrum of needs of all children.

131

The consequences of the further divisions of responsibility, as can be so easily identified in many schools is that teachers seem to be expected to take on more and more additions to their daily load, whilst fewer are actually involved in the decisions that increase their load and dominate their working lives. In very few schools does a coherent and serious staff development programme exist. It is not normally considered a task of school management and therefore becomes an end of term jamboree or a scramble to add another sentence to the next job application form.

To reverse what is happening can be creative and productive. It is not that teachers are resisting change or challenges, they cannot respond wholeheartedly without the necessary adjustments to the management practice of senior staff further supported by a deflection of resources for training.

The great advantage of opening up the whole question of education to public debate, of both a political and parochial type, is that schools have been able, or obliged, to look beyond their own boundaries and be open to influence from a number of different directions. When schools do respond by removing the shackles of systems, take on board *genuine* staff development and the search for a 'whole child' approach, a much more creative approach to education can result and the whole professional being of teachers takes on a new meaning. The move towards such an existence does not imply revolution or radical change, but it does require a greater awareness of senior staff to focus the operation of the school upon classroom practice and teacher cooperation coupled with coherent and sensitive supporting strategies.

c) Traditions and Established Patterns

Before moving towards teachers working in teams, it will be necessary to examine some of the time honoured practices of schools that will block real teacher involvement. One can already hear statements, "it won't work here because . . .", "the timetable won't allow . . .", etc. It is important to question some of these time honoured practices and assess whether the reasons for establishing them still apply, or have they just become a useful administrative protective mechanism?

Identifying stumbling blocks

i) Why do we divide the secondary school day into small segments and so produce a diet of 'bits' which are controlled by a ritual of bells and buzzers? Moving on from one activity to the next without the opportunity to get really involved can often produce conflicts of learning for children and goes against most normal learning processes.

ii) What is the dominating thinking behind a curriculum that focuses on small amounts of learning time repeated at frequent intervals? Is it to enhance the learning process? - Or is it a compromise arrangement to satisfy the differing needs of subject specialism, the balance of which we dare not disturb?

iii) Why do we concentrate on a weekly timetable that is repetitive, without using our combined resources for at least some of the time establishing different opportunities? Why not a full day to concentrate on one area of the curriculum, say once a month? Or a whole week when children, teachers and possibly others can work together on a particular project, or spend some time together away from the school campus?

iv) Is it essential always to structure the school on year groups? Is there advantage to be gained, for at least some of the time, from enabling different age groups to work together? (We do so often quite naturally during the rest of our lives when a common interest is the bond.)

v) Why do we presume to be the only educator within the experience of the child's daily life? All schools have round them a community, of which they are a part, that has an enormous resource of expertise and experience if only we are brave enough to take advantage of its existence.

It is up to the senior staff team to question the existence of the boundaries created by the established practice and examine the motives that lead to the large expenditure of energy used to protect them. Can some of that energy be redirected?

Curriculum Involvement

Once a school moves towards the establishment of teams of teachers becoming involved in curriculum development and responding to structural changes that result from such a move, a more natural working environment evolves and much more purpose is associated to the whole question of staff development. As a member of a team, trusted with the task of curriculum development, the emphasis of the role of the teacher is towards classroom management with an expectation of sharing experience and actual practice. The energies and expertise of senior staff can be concentrated in supporting groups to enhance that practice and organise development programmes. Because they are immersed in the development of learning strategies, in-service programmes can be directed towards increasing the awareness of teachers so enabling them to handle the development task. As a consequence, teachers themselves will be able to identify their own training needs. It is at this point that resources for training outside school can take a more meaningful role in teacher education and training than has hitherto been the case, as training becomes an integral part of teacher development and not a simple appendage.

Possible Strategies within Secondary Schools

- based on establishing 'teams' of teachers - with a challenge to take responsibility for their working.

A simple model to harness that energy could be: (with all staff being a member of at least one curriculum and one service team)

```
            (11-14) : (14-16) : (16+-90)
                    :         :
SERVICE TEAMS ___    CURRICULUM TEAM          _____
                    :         :
SERVICE TEAMS ___    CURRICULUM TEAM
                    :         :
SERVICE TEAMS ___    CURRICULUM TEAM
                    :         :
SERVICE TEAMS ___    CURRICULUM TEAM
                    :         :
SERVICE TEAMS ___    CURRICULUM TEAM
                    :         :
SERVICE TEAMS ___    CURRICULUM TEAM
                    :         :
SERVICE TEAMS ___    CURRICULUM TEAM
                    :         :  etc
              ↑     :    ↑    :   ↑
                CURRICULUM GROUPS
```

Curriculum Team:

An effective grouping for appropriate subject links, e.g. Humanities/Science/Languages/Creative Arts/etc. Posts of responsibility can then be allied to team leadership in curriculum development and evaluation for an age group.

Curriculum Group:

The coordination of *whole school* curriculum focus, the team crossing curriculum boundaries.

Service Team:

Teams which are structured to take responsibility on a whole school front for health and social development, environment, careers, reprographics, evaluation, profiling, etc.

A school management structure based on the 'whole school' approach becomes possible with teachers involved in the full educational experience of the individual child and not just a fragmented part. A revolution is not needed to stimulate this change, it is quite feasible within our current institutions and with our current structures.

Developing a Different Approach - the effect on training

Once the prime task for senior staff of creating greater teacher involvement is commenced, the consequent development takes on a predictable and logical sequence. A prerequisite will be an acknowledged staff development programme where all teachers can know that their individual performance and future are sufficiently important to be recognised and that someone is able to produce an honest and professional appraisal.

In-service training, both school based and as organised by external agencies, can be managed to support teachers through the development taking place in their own schools and to increase awareness in all aspects of teaching. From such a process, teachers will inevitably become more conscious of the gaps in their own expertise and will be able to contribute to identifying their own training needs.

Those responsible for training will then be in a position to respond to training needs as opposed to the current stance which determines a diet of courses and then offers a menu on a take it or leave it basis. The fact that courses of training are normally oversubscribed should not be read as a message of satisfaction for those responsible for training without first determining teachers' motives for participating and measuring any consequent gain to their schools.

If training is not a response to teachers' needs, as determined by teachers involved in their work and appropriately placed to measure that need, then training becomes no more than a justification of the cost of budget expenditure. Training that takes teachers exclusively out of school will always invoke from some colleagues the jibe that they are 'on

135

holiday' or 'away from the action', since the relevance and advantage to their own institution cannot always be perceived or justified. How much more powerful if those colleagues are involved in identifying and contributing to the menu . . . .

With curriculum responsibility back where it should be at classroom management level and with support strategies following that basic principle, the school rapidly gains a sense of purpose, energy and dynamism from which learning emerges as a highly creative experience. Much involvement and cooperation becomes possible, false boundaries are demolished and the whole concept of the community of the school becomes more than an idealistic dream. The starting point of the immersion of the teacher into real involvement is a simple but brave step to take. Once taken, the effect on children's education is positive and dramatic. All children come within the consciousness of teachers and thus the need to over-identify one particular group becomes unnecessary and focus on the individual is the norm.

Chapter Twelve

A NATIONAL INITIATIVE : THE SCOTTISH EXPERIENCE

Marion Blythman

Abstract

After a two year survey of remedial work in Scottish schools,
HM Inspectors in their report, "The Education of Pupils with
Learning Difficulties in Primary and Secondary Schools in
Scotland", referred to hereafter as the Progress Report,
proposed that the response to such difficulties should be
planned on a whole school basis because the range of learning
difficulties is so wide and their nature so complex that it is
too much to ask that they be tackled by the provision of
remedial teachers alone. The report emphasised that the major
source of difficulty lay in the curriculum and how it is
presented. At this time, this was a new and radical approach.

    A series of seminars held by the Inspectorate followed,
involving Education Authority personnel at senior level,
College of Education, advisers, headteachers and promoted staff
in schools in discussion and debate.   This culminated in an
acceptance of the principles enunciated in the report and in an
agreement that new forms of in-service training should be
devised to meet the needs of staff involved in operating the
new roles of the remedial specialist, specified in the Progress
Report, particularly consultancy and cooperative teaching.

    The case study which follows describes how this was put
into operation at national level, and at local level involving
one College of Education and one Education Authority, and
presents a model for staff development based on an analysis of
the changing needs of pupils, and teachers, and the
organisations within which they operate.

The Progress Report and Others

Two important reports, published in 1978, both expressed a
need for a broader definition of pupils who experience learn-

137

ing difficulties. The Warnock Report, which covered the UK, estimated that one child in five was likely to have special educational needs and would therefore require special educational provision at some point in his/her school career. However, later in the same year a Progress Report of HM Inspectors of Schools (Scotland) emphasised that learning difficulties embraced a greater number of pupils than that normally thought of as requiring remedial education, which itself was to be given a wider definition. The Progress Report made, inter alia, the following main points:

(a) There is a range and diversity of learning difficulties which goes well beyond the failure to master the basic skills of reading and computation, and there is, therefore, a need for a wider interpretation of remedial education than that currently found in most schools.

(b) The curriculum is at once the main cause and 'potential' cure of many learning difficulties. The design of the curriculum, the way it is differentiated to match the varied abilities of pupils and above all the adoption of appropriate methodologies are of the utmost importance.

(c) The class teacher in the primary school and the subject teacher in the secondary school have the prime responsibility for dealing with learning difficulties. Remedial education is, therefore, the concern of all teachers, and any response to learning difficulties must be planned on a whole school basis.

(d) A new role has to be found for the specialist remedial teacher which is seen to be 'unique' and fits into this whole school policy. This role must be multi-purpose and was seen to encompass four main strands, i.e.

   (i) acting as a consultant to staff and members of the school management team;

   (ii) providing personal tuition and support for pupils with learning difficulties in the early processes of language and computation;

   (iii) in cooperation with class and subject teachers providing tutorial and supportive help in their normal classes to pupils with learning difficulties in the later stages of these processes;

   (iv) providing, arranging for, or contributing to special services within the school for pupils with temporary learning difficulties.

138

This report represented a new and radical change in
educational thinking in Scotland at the time of publication,
claiming as it does that the wider definition of remedial
education could include up to 50 per cent of the whole school
population. It is both interesting and informative to examine
the strategies for dissemination and implementation which
followed and assess to what extent they have been successful
and therefore provide a generalisable model for translation of
national policies into action at school and teacher level.

A recent report from the National Committee for In-Service
Training (Scotland) to the Secretary of State for Scotland
makes the following statement in a paper which has been put out
for discussion.

"There are three contexts through which staff development
operates. Firstly, there is the school context. This includes
individual members of staff, the functional groups operating
within the school and the school management.   Secondly, there
is the education authority context.   Thirdly, there is the
national context, comprising the Secretary of State and the
SED, the National Committee for In-Service Training and the
College of Education and the Universities.   We recommend the
establishment, within each of these contexts, of clearly
identified arrangements through which the processes of staff
development can be carried out.   We would emphasise that we do
not wish to see the creation of a complicated and bureaucratic
system of reporting . . . . Our essential plea is that those
responsible . . . should adopt a system in which teachers are
encouraged to participate."

National Initiatives

A series of seminars followed the publication of the Progress
Report characterised by the presentation by the HMI of actual
evidence, in the form of pupils' work, which had been derived
from an extensive survey of provision for pupils with learning
difficulties gathered by the inspectorate over a two year
period. That these seminars were influential and convincing is
without question, encompassing as they did Local Authority
personnel, Colleges of Education and school staffs and
management teams. It is, however, worth noting that the survey
had highlighted both good and bad practice.   While it was
generally agreed that in many instances the concept of
remedial education had been too narrowly defined, it is also
clear that the main thrusts of the report reflected initiatives
on the part of some remedial staff and also policy development
found in certain schools.   While undoubtedly the strategy of
dissemination involving key people was crucial, the
timing was right for it was becoming evident that the

pedagogic patterns had begun to change and a climate of opinion was emerging which provided a favourable context for many of the conclusions drawn by the report.

It was also unacceptable that the new policies would be imposed on any of the providing agencies, and it was clear that Local Authorities, training institutions and schools would need to work out their own policies in the light of local circumstances. Changes of the nature proposed were going to demand much of authorities, training institutions and teachers, who would all need time for assimilation and enactment. It was recognised also that about this time many authorities had either produced reports concerned with provision for pupils with learning difficulties or were in process of so doing and that any national initiatives would have to take these factors into account and build on work already undertaken.

The first round of seminars produced a surprising level of consensus for a race as schismatic as the Scots are reputed to be and it was generally agreed that the main recommendations of the Progress Report could be accepted, that the key to implementation lay in in-service training and that schools, colleges and local authorities needed to get together in order to involve a workable strategy. This was seen to be no mean task since the implication of the Progress Report was that *all* members of staff would need to be involved if the idea of a whole school policy was to become a reality. It was also seen as important that this specific aspect of in-service training should not be regarded as a discrete credentialising qualification confined to a limited number of 'experts' but that the ideas and implications of the findings of the survey and the report should inform and pervade other in-service courses, particularly those on curriculum and management.

In developing the national strategy over a period of years certain basic principles have been established when in-service training designed to change policy and provision is being planned in a systematic way.

(a) The right people must be trained first. In the case of the Progress Report it was decided that these should be the 'enablers', mainly holders of promoted posts, for without their willingness and commitment, their ability to plan the curriculum, organise their resources and deploy their staff, little progress would be made in schools.

(b) Staff development activities must have a sound practical basis at school level but should be planned and coordinated at school management and local authority levels. While in-service training is something which schools themselves have to do and seems to be most successful when needs are identified and priorities are established at that level it was emphasised that cognisance must also be taken of the full range of agencies available including the teaching unions.

(c) Schools do need help from outside agencies - particularly the training institutions who, in turn, need staff with recent, valid experience and the expertise to mount the kinds of courses or offer the kind of help needed by schools.

College of Education Initiatives

In 1980, the Committee of Principals, which coordinates, at national level, the work of the individual colleges of education, set up the Advisory Committee on Pupils with Learning Difficulties, part of whose remit was to consider the implications of the Progress Report for the training of teachers who would be particularly involved with the larger group of pupils, many of whose difficulties stemmed from the curriculum and how it is presented and whose needs would mainly be met within the ordinary school and who might, in fact, account for up to 50 per cent of the total school population. This advisory committee included a broad range of interests including representatives of the colleges, the local authorities, professional associations and teachers' unions. All discussion was held in an open way, the minutes of the committee made available to all who were interested and the representatives of the various bodies charged with the responsibility of transmitting the findings of the committee to their organisations and of keeping the committee aware of the views of their constituent bodies. Therefore, at each stage of the discussion about the response to the Progress Report and the new forms of training the Advisory Committee was involved in a process of open debate which many felt to be fairly unique at the time. It is interesting to note that the guidelines for the new B.Ed pre- and in-service courses in Scotland have been developed along similar lines.

This committee proposed a new advanced diploma designed to reflect the radical changes in attitudes towards the education of pupils with learning difficulties and which was to be the distinctive qualification for Scottish teachers working in this field in both primary and secondary schools. It produced GENERAL REQUIREMENTS for the training, detailed below, and a checklist, available from the Committee of Principals, which set out the criteria against which the appropriateness of any course proposal from individual colleges could be evaluated. It was recognised however that although these criteria would be binding there would be different ways of realising the aims and that college based course planning teams would be expected to put forward different selections of learning experience designed to meet identified local needs.

Paper 1 - National Advisory Committee
"General Requirements for the DLD Course (December 1980)

1. The *central aim* of the course must be to produce teachers able to fulfil the multi-purpose role, and equipped with appropriate skills, knowledge and attitudes.

2. Appropriate *knowledge* may be examined in relation to each role under four headings:

   2.1 *Curricular,* referring to the pupils' courses in school, and the problems they raise.

   2.2 *Social* in a broad sense, referring to all relevant groups, e.g. the family, the schools, supporting agencies.

   2.3 *Psychological,* referring to the mental and emotional processes of pupils.

   2.4 *Pedagogical,* referring to the processes of teaching, and the problems they raise.

3. Appropriate *general skills* will include:

   3.1 Expertise in the processes of consultancy,

   3.2 Expertise in working with individual pupils with learning difficulty.

   3.3 Ability to cooperate with colleagues and others.

   3.4 Ability to formulate and maintain a broad view of the curriculum.

   3.5 Skill in providing, contributing to or arranging for special services for pupils with temporary learning difficulties.

4. Appropriate *attitudes* in Diplomates will include:

   4.1 Positive sympathy with the needs of children of learning difficulties.

4.2 A belief that fundamental change and success are possible.

4.3 Respect of the uniqueness of each pupil's personality.

4.4 Professionalism and discretion in dealing with and discussing individual difficulties.

4.5 Willingness to cooperate with colleagues, parents and supporting agencies.

5. In reference to each strand in the Diplomate's role, these matters of knowledge, skills and attitudes are worked out in greater detail in the accompanying *Checklist.*

Provision, Administration and Duration of Courses

1. The course will be offered by Colleges of Education, either individually or in cooperation.

   1.1 Each course however must draw widely on the experience and expertise of *practitioners* in schools and other areas (not only educational).

   1.2 The Course should be *planned, organised and run* by a broadly based group, including representatives of several college departments and local teachers and administrators, and chaired by a member of the higher administrative staff of the College.

   1.3 Since extensive resources will be required in each course, it may be necessary for some colleges to *combine* their effort.

2. The *duration* of the course, if it is offered full time, shall be the equivalent of one college session.

   2.1 *Starting dates* need not coincide with those of the school or college session.

   2.2 Consideration may be given to *part-time equivalents.*

   2.3 Consideration may be given to a *modular structure.*

3. The emphasis in the course shall be strongly *practical.* This will entail:

   3.1 A substantial contribution by practising teachers and administrators in the planning and teaching

143

of the course. *Credibility,* based on practical experience, must be possessed by all major contributors.

3.2 A substantial proportion of the course devoted to *school experience* and to specific examples of pupils' learning difficulties. It is suggested that approximately 14 weeks be spent in school-based work, which must be structured.

3.3 The course must not be 'overtaught'. Not more than 60 per cent of the course in College shall be occupied by lectures, seminars and tutorials, the rest being devoted to assignments and timetabled private study.

3.4 School experience shall occur in *at least two schools.*

3.5 The College of Education course must be based on actual case studies.

4. The course may be offered in *primary* or in *secondary* education.

4.1 Where a college is able to muster the necessary resources, it may wish to offer both courses, with certain areas of *overlap*, possibly on a modular basis. Each individual course, however, must concern itself mainly with the problems specific to the primary *or* the secondary school.

4.2 Once the DLD has been established, the feasibility should be explored of mounting a third type of course, concentrating on the problems of 10 to 14 year olds.

4.3 Similarly, the feasibility may be explored of diplomates adding a primary to a secondary qualification, or vice versa.

5. The course should maintain *links with other college courses*, including those in special education, the UPA and B.Ed but such links must not be allowed to weaken or distort the aims of the DLD course.

Selection for the Course

1. Priority in allocating places on the course should be given to *teachers seconded* by their employing authority.

2. The *responsibility for selecting* such teachers will rest with the authority, but a scheme should be established

for consultation between authority and college. Selection for secondment will not carry with it any guarantee of future promotion.

3. *Criteria for selection* must include:

   3.1 *Extensive experience in normal education,* and with children of all levels and kinds of ability.

   3.2 Success as a *practising teacher.*

   3.3 Evidence of thinking on the wider aspects and problems of the *school curriculum.*

   3.4 Registration in the sector (primary or secondary) in which the candidate will operate. Exceptionally, however, evidence of substantial experience and success in the other sector may be accepted instead.

   3.5 The ability to establish *good personal relationships* with pupils and colleagues.

4. Where all candidates meet these criteria, priority in allocating places should be given to teachers holding a qualification in *remedial education.*

Content of the Course:

1. The content of each course (primary or secondary) shall include the elements specified in the accompanying check-list.

Assessment and Validation:

1. Each course proposal must put forward suggested arrangements for assessment, including the employment of *external examiners* and some indication of where they are likely to be found.

2. The Committee of Principals should maintain an *Advisory Committee* on the DLD to advise it (and the Secretary of State) on the acceptability of college proposals.

3. In considering proposals by colleges for a DLD we are informed that the SED will operate the criteria listed in Appendix B.

Credit for Existing Qualifications:

1. Since the DLD is based on a *fundamentally new approach,* it is impossible for any candidate to have completed already

all the elements constituting the award.

2. However, the holders of certain existing qualifications, for example, those in:

>   Remedial Education
>   Early Education
>   Upper Primary Education
>   Certain OU Courses

may have covered part of the syllabus for the new Diploma. The Advisory Committee will consider schemes for the award of *credits*."

The principles set out in the General Requirements point towards a collaborative model in which there is a recognition that staff development is at the heart of educational progress but that it must also meet the needs of the individual teacher, the pupils they teach and the organisations in which they operate. The analysis of need should take place through a process of consultation and collaboration where all the needs are taken into account within a framework which has been generally agreed through a policy of participation, debate and discussion. Viewed in this way, the vexed question of academic autonomy fades in significance and appears to be theoretical since the model comprises levels of professional interaction and cooperation which can be detailed at various stages but which should combine to form a dynamic and integrated system. Such a system must be flexible enough to be applied to all schools and local authorities but at the same time provide broad enough guidelines so that individual schools, colleges and local authorities can adapt the model to meet their new priorities and their own specific requirements.

Local Authority Initiatives

Simultaneously developments were taking place at Local Authority level following on the conclusions and recommendations of a joint inspectorate/education authority seminar which had been held in 1979. It had been recommended there that a senior administrator who already had wider curricular responsibilities should be assigned the specific tasks of coordinating and directing the authority's policy on pupils with learning difficulties. There is little doubt that, where this has been the position, and the person appointed committed and in a position of some power, that the support and guidance provided by such a senior member of the education authority had had a decisive effect on the identification of need and implementation of a coordinated policy for in-service training. It had been further suggested at national level that the education authorities should prepare guidelines for

schools. The guidelines would offer general advice on differ-
entiating the content, pace of learning and gradient of
difficulty when introducing new ideas and concepts into the
curriculum and on ways of devising methods of teaching appropriate to the ability of individual pupils. It was recognised
that this task was not without its difficulties since,
traditionally in Scotland, headteachers had enjoyed a great
deal of independence and autonomy in devising curricula. It
was further recognised that the authorities themselves had
a significant role to play in the dissemination of the
national policies. They were encouraged to hold a series of
meetings with their headteachers where the evidence from the
survey would be presented and discussed, and headteachers
'invited' to consider how they were going to go about the
implementation of the findings of the Progress Report in their
own schools.

By June 1980, the Fife Regional Authority had produced
the following paper for the headteachers of their primary
schools. A similar paper was issued to secondary schools in
the same region about the same time.

Paper 2 - Fife Regional Council Education Committee (June 1980)
"The Education of Pupils with Learning Difficulties

The Education Authority, having carefully considered the
implications of the recent SED report on this subject, has
decided to issue guidelines on how the education of pupils
with learning difficulties should be approached in primary
schools. What is being insisted upon by the Authority is a
commitment by schools and evidence of a well considered
strategy to bring about the required improvements. Copies
of the guidelines are attached for all promoted staff.

Headteachers are expected to make substantial progress
over the next three years towards drawing up and implementing
their own school policies along the lines advocated in the
guidelines. The Authority will mount in-service training and
provide other help and advise to school staff during this
period to assist headteachers in their task.

By July 1981 the following targets should be met by headteachers.

(a) All schools should have a written policy on the education
    of pupils with learning difficulties. The school staff
    as a whole should have an opportunity of contributing
    to its formulation and be aware of their individual and
    corporate roles regarding its implementation throughout
    the school.

147

(b)   The resources of the school should be assessed in detail as to their adequacy in providing an appropriate education for all pupils.

(c)   The in-service training requirements of all staff should be assessed and staff meetings held to discuss, explain and clarify the contents of the SED report and the Authority's guidelines.

(d)   All new curriculum guidance should be discussed with staff, particularly in relation to the differentiation required for pupils with learning difficulties.

(e)   All difficulties standing in the way of full implementation of the school policy should be identified.

It is emphasised that the above targets are minimum objectives and it is acknowledged that in some aspects schools may achieve further progress. The setting of these minimum targets should not discourage schools from moving more quickly towards the 1983 objectives.

By July of 1983 schools are expected to have realised the following targets.

(a)   The existence in all schools of an adequate range of resources to provide all pupils with an appropriate education.

(b)   The teaching of the basic skills to pupils by the use of group and individual methods.

(c)   The full implementation of a sound assessment policy, with associated record keeping and remedial action.

(d)   The full implementation of curriculum guidelines particularly in Language Arts, Mathematics and Environmental Studies with special attention being given to the careful grading of work for all pupils.

(e)   Where remedial teachers exist they should be working along the lines advocated in the guidelines, being involved with class teachers in a whole school approach to the education of children with learning difficulties.

The guidelines to this circular should be discussed with promoted staff and remedial teachers in readiness for the initial seminars for promoted staff which will be organised by the Authority during the first term to allow staff to discuss in detail the guidelines and their implementation.

These seminars will herald a three year programme of training for staff directly related to the education of pupils with learning difficulties."

Clearly these papers show a degree of commitment to national policy and a combination of leadership and direction which is quite unequivocal. Such arrangements are aimed to enable the education authority to bring about innovation, and establish fundamental changes in practice and provision. The Fife guidelines, even at this early stage, for two years after the publication of the Progress Report is not long in educational terms, have a degree of specificity which ensures that headteachers and staffs are left in no doubt about the way in which the authority is intending to move, and are provided with details of the in-service activities appropriate to the development of the new policies.

Teacher Initiatives

The Progress Report had not been universally welcomed by the teaching profession, particularly those who were working in remedial classes and departments. There was indeed a fair degree of resentment about what was regarded as implied criticism of their efforts, a high degree of anxiety, and considerable uncertainty about their future as 'remedial teachers'. Obviously the teachers felt that the work they had been doing was being undervalued and while some felt confident about adapting the new multi-purpose roles, the majority obviously felt that they were being asked to venture out into uncharted territory and could see the dangers and pitfalls of so doing without the right kind of support and in-service back-up.

Perhaps the fact that Scotland is a fairly small country in population terms was a critical feature at this stage for the word of change soon gets round and, apart from anything else, curiosity and novelty play their part. The Educational Institute of Scotland (EIS) which is the main teachers' union, and the Scottish Association of Remedial Education (SARE), also got into the act and fortunately both endorsed the main recommendations of the Progress Report. A series of well-attended open meetings was convened, some of which were stormy to say the least. These provided a forum where the pros and cons of the new policies were well and truly thrashed out. This is where the original strategy of working through key people from a variety of contexts demonstrated its value, for a typical line up at these meetings would comprise an HMI, an education authority senior representative, a College of Education lecturer and a member of the appropriate teachers' body. It was an essential part of the whole process that opportunities would be provided where reservations could be aired openly and the main issues settled. There was a measure of real conflict which had to be resolved between the staff development needs as defined at national level and the aspirations of many of the individual teachers who attended these meetings. It seemed however that the time was ripe for, on the whole, there was agreement that the old ways were in need of change. While there remain unresolved questions and a few pockets of resistance, now somewhat isolated, the teachers have moved to accept the new roles and responsibilities and seem keen to put themselves forward for the new forms of training.

By 1982 the first diploma courses were being mounted, having been planned by Colleges of Education in close cooperation with local authority representatives in accordance with the General Requirements. These had, of course, set up a collaborative model which in effect meant that a totally joint planning exercise had to be undertaken. It is to the credit of the local authorities that at a time when financial problems were looming large and staffing levels deteriorating, they were more than willing to give the time necessary to play their full part. It is also to the credit of the Scottish colleges that they departed from their traditional stance of 'sole providers' and again, in a situation where staffing levels were deteriorating and 'new blood' something for the future, were able to realise the enormous benefits to be derived from joint planning of and shared responsibility for in-service courses. The paper which follows, dated June 1982, shows the advanced stage reached by Fife Region through the phased programme of implementation involving, as it did, a planned and detailed programme of in-service training for all staff.

Paper 3 - Fife Regional Council Education Committee (June 1982) "The Education of Pupils with Learning Difficulties in Secondary Schools: Development Programme

1. Introduction

The purpose of this report is:

(1) To describe briefly the steps taken so far by the Authority and the schools to implement the main conclusions of the Progress Report by HM Inspector of Schools. Headteachers are reminded of the Authority's commitment to the main themes of the Progress Report and of its intention to introduce the required changes in a phased programme. Schools are, therefore, asked to review progress and to ensure that the changes so

far requested by the Director of Education are being comprehensively implemented.

It is recognised that considerable progress has been made in some schools along the lines suggested and in keeping with the in-service courses which have been provided for Rectors, Assistant Rectors (Curriculum) and certain Principal Teachers.

(2) To indicate the further steps which will be required of all schools during session 1982/83, so that planning and discussion can be undertaken in good time for more fundamental changes to be initiated *for August 1983.*

2. The Current Position: Phased Programme of Implementation

(1) The HM Inspector's Progress Report dealing with the above subject was published in March 1978. Following its publication and due consideration of its main conclusions, this Education Authority issued its own Policy Guidelines in March 1980 (circular 135/80/DMcN/FC). The major theme of the guidelines was that the main responsibility for dealing with pupils' learning difficulties would now rest with the subject class teacher who would operate within a coherent school policy with remedial teachers widening their role to work as specialists providing a learning support service throughout the subject departments of the secondary school.

(2) Seminars and meetings were held with headteachers and senior promoted staff to discuss the Authority's Guidelines and the implications for its schools. It was agreed that the changes requested would have to be introduced gradually, and that remedial teachers would require to be trained for the difficult, exacting and major role of consultancy: some remedial staff would require to be replaced or redeployed.

It was, therefore, decided to embark upon a phased programme of implementation with feasible targets set for each school session.

Requirements were as follows:

Session 1980/82

(a) The establishment of a school committee to supervise this development under the Chairmanship of a member of the Board of Studies - preferably the Assistant Rector Curriculum.

(b) The discontinuance of separate and segregated remedial classes or tutorial groups specially created for the purpose. It was accepted that tuition on an individual withdrawal basis from normal mainstream classes would be necessary for certain pupils.

(c) The inclusion of the in-service period at the start of the session 1980/82 of a substantial element on pupils with Learning Difficulties informing the teaching staff of the Policy Guidelines and the implications.

(d) The ensuring that appropriate information would be received and utilised about the learning difficulties of pupils at the transfer stage through direct contact between the schools.

(e) The conducting by the Authority of in-service courses for staff, particularly promoted staff who would be responsible for managing the changes in the schools. Assistant Rectors/Principal Teachers/Advisers would have an opportunity to attend the Moray House Course "Towards an Appropriate Education". In addition the Remedial Adviser would work in the secondary sector only, for the next few years.

(3) The Director of Education issued a Paper in December 1980 (copy of an in-service talk given by the Senior Deputy Director of Education) in which guidance was given on:

(a) Conducting a stocktaking exercise to re-appraise existing arrangements (para 2(1) page 3).

(b) Tackling, on a whole school basis, problem areas in the classroom (para 2(2) page 5).

In addition, it was indicated that schools should *begin* to think about piloting changes in curriculum and methodology in the first two years of secondary education. Timetabling changes would be needed to reduce the number of subjects studied at any one time and the number of teachers with whom pupils come into contact (para 2(2) page 5 of the Paper and para 3.8 of the Authority's Guidelines).

152

(4) During the current school session the following progress was planned:

Session 1981/82

(a) Eight remedial teachers to be selected and seconded for the new one year full-time Diploma in Learning Difficulties Course at Moray House College of Education.

(b) Further in-service work to be conducted with Principal Teachers of remedial education and mathematics and with remedial teachers.

(c) School Committees to produce their own policy statements in keeping with the Authority's Guidelines and the HM Inspector's Report, including policies for identifying and dealing with learning difficulties within subject departments.

(d) A Regional Working Party to be set up to provide guidance on companion teaching and the curriculum to be offered to certain pupils withdrawn on an individual tutorial basis.

(e) The Director of Education to begin appropriate consultation about the replacement or redeployment of existing remedial teachers who would be unable to meet the new requirements for the new Diploma in Learning Difficulties."

By 1983 the new diploma courses were well established, had changed their nomenclature in order to come into line with the Education (Scotland) Act 1981 and as the following extract shows, had become an essential part of Local Authority strategy for implementation of the nationally developed policies.

Paper 4 - Fife Regional Council Education Committee (December (1983)
"The Diploma in Special Educational Needs (Non-Recorded Pupils)

1. The Diploma in Special Educational Needs (Non-Recorded Pupils) is designed to be the distinctive qualification course for teachers specialising in the new multi-purpose roles of the Remedial Specialist which were laid down in the Inspectorate's PLD Report and which have been accepted for implementation by Fife Education Authority. This course was formerly called the Diploma in Learning Difficulties or DLD.

2. Fife Education Authority regards this Diploma as an essential professional qualification course for future Remedial Specialists and priority is to be given to Remedial Specialists in making nominations for places on the course.

3. The course is offered by a number of colleges of education in Scotland both as a full-time course extending over one college session and as a full-time equivalent course extending over one and a half college sessions.

4. Moray House College of Education has run this course from 1981 and Fife Education Authority has seconded eight members of staff to the course in each of the sessions 1981-82, 1982-83, 1983-84.

5. It is proposed that similar numbers of staff will be seconded to undertake this course in forthcoming sessions.

6. The Moray House course has the status of an advanced postgraduate diploma at a level considerably above that of initial teacher training. It has been approved by the Scottish Education Department, the National Advisory Committee of the Scottish Colleges of Education and the Committee for National Academic Awards.

7. As Remedial Specialists are seconded to undertake the course, temporary posts will be created for replacement teachers to fill the resulting vacancies for a session. This arrangement is intended to ensure continuity of work in the school concerned. It has also proved to be of substantial benefit in acting as a potential means of recruitment for future Remedial Specialists.

8. The post of Remedial Specialist and this Diploma is regarded by the Education Authority as one possible route for promotion to posts of senior responsibility."

By 1984 diploma courses were established in most of the Scottish colleges, at both primary and secondary level and increasing numbers of the new remedial specialists were appearing in schools. As noted earlier, in order to get SED approval, all courses have had to meet the criteria laid down by the National Advisory Committee yet currently show a healthy degree of diversity in the way they set about meeting local needs within these constraints. College staff, on the whole, have appreciated the guidance which has been provided. An inter-college system of communication has been established and now there is a regular exchange of views about past, present and future developments in all matters to do with pupils with learning difficulties. Seminars and conferences have been held at national level through the good offices of the Committee of Principals, where course planning teams have discussed common issues and have shared problems and solutions arising from the evaluation of the individual courses in an open and discursive atmosphere. Colleges of Education, like schools, have come to an acceptance that if the spirit and philosophy of the Progress Report are to be translated into action, they must inform and pervade all the courses and not just those aimed at teachers whose prime responsibility will be with pupils with learning difficulties as can be seen from the following statement from Moray House College of Education in Edinburgh.

Paper 5

"Moray House College of Education
Board of Studies Policy Paper 179
(Agreed 16 May 1984)

The Education of Pupils with Learning Difficulties

. . .

B. College Policy

3. Basic to the philosophy of the college is the belief that teachers should be enabled, through the nature of their training, to meet the educational needs of the broad range of children who are found in the mainstream schools and classes with the exception of the very small percentage of pupils whose educational difficulties or needs are such that their teachers require additional training, i.e. Diploma in Special Education Needs (Recorded and Non-Recorded Pupils - Primary and Secondary).

4. College policy is based on a view that there are many factors which affect how pupils learn and perform in school. In the broadest sense these are physiological, psychological, socio-logical, political and economic which together influence the child, the school, the content of the curriculum and how it is presented. Rather than concentrate on the child as the only source of the problem of school failures, the training offered should develop in teachers an awareness of and sensitivity to the effects of the factors specified above and how they help or hinder progress.

5. The general approach of the college is that the thrust of the training should reflect a move away from a passive determinism to an optimistic belief in the power of the school, the teacher and the pupil working together to make the learning process appropriate and effective.

6. Specifically, all teachers should be aware of the broad range of learning difficulties experienced by pupils in school, including those generated by the school and therefore within the sphere of influence of class and subject teachers including:

    (a) inappropriate curriculum and methodology;

    (b) a failure to teach study skills;

    (c) lack of awareness of problems related to language of instruction, terminology and other specialised language demands and to instruction not being in the first language of the pupil;

    (d) many changes of teacher and poor timetable;

    (e) lack of awareness of the difficulties faced by pupils in coming to terms with concepts and processes;

    (f) an attitude which restricts the contexts of learning and which does not encourage or enable the child to play a significant part in the process of learning;

    (g) lack of awareness of the cultural, political and socio-economic backgrounds and contexts of the pupils.

7. The training must help teachers to identify:

    (a) those difficulties which can be dealt with by them through a differentiated curriculum;

    (b) those difficulties which can still be dealt with within the classroom but with additional support;

    (c) the small percentage for which specialised intervention is necessary.

8. To sum up, teachers should know when and where to call for help and have knowledge of the kinds of help available in the varieties of educational provision and from the range of support services, particularly that offered by remedial specialists trained to operate the four roles specified in the HMI Progress Report (1978).

9. To achieve this, the whole curriculum of professional training in practical and theoretical courses must be conducted in an awareness of the philosophy enunciated

in this policy statement. While there are aspects of
knowledge and specific skills and resources which will
be particularly relevant to the needs of pupils with
learning difficulties, the main aims in this area will
be to emphasise that the class teacher in the primary
school and the subject teacher in the secondary school
have the prime responsibility for dealing with learning
difficulties and that meeting the difficulties and educational needs of pupils is the concern of all teachers as
part of a policy planned on a whole school basis. The
design of the school curriculum, the way it is differentiated to match the ranging abilities of the pupils and
the adoption of appropriate methodologies are therefore
of the utmost importance and as such must be reflected
in every aspect of in-service training.

. . . ."

Conclusions

It is not easy to evaluate the long-term effects of this
particular development or to estimate objectively to what
extent the strategies used for dissemination and action have
contributed to improvements in practice and provision. In
Scotland it would be difficult to separate the outcome of this
activity from the other developments in curriculum and assessment that have followed on the publication of the Munn and
Dunning Reports and the more recent Action Plan which deal
with the education of the 16-18 year olds. There is nevertheless a strong impression that the education of pupils with
learning difficulties has become much more of a central
concern of teachers, schools and colleges and that education
authorities have been induced and encouraged to adopt new
styles of organisation designed to produce more appropriate
education for *all* the pupils in the school. They have also
proved themselves, on the whole, to be willing to support
these through the provision of resources mainly directed
towards in-service training. New forms of training have been
devised to conform to national standards and are, at the same
time, flexible enough to match the capacity of individual
colleges to meet and fulfil the local needs of schools and
education authorities.

    Within a Scottish context, the same kind of model has
been used in the development of more recent initiatives
related to in-service training and curriculum development.
It is interesting therefore to reflect on the elements which
were novel in their time but with hindsight still judged to
be effective. Among these one can list:

157

1. The new policies enunciated in the Progress Report were based on an extensive survey by the HMI which highlighted, in a factual way, the need for change.

2. The time was ripe for the best of practice observed in the schools was showing the way things might go.

3. The dissemination of the findings involved seminars with individual teachers, school management teams, trainers, senior education authority personnel and HMI.

4. The seminars were convincing because the hard evidence derived from actual examples of pupils' work was presented and the participants invited to make their own inferences and draw their own conclusions. This seemed more effective than pious exhortation and, in addition, gave a sense of partnership between the inspectorate and the various audiences involved.

5. The main aim of the dissemination was to stimulate action through involvement of personnel at school, training institution, education authority and national levels in specific tasks related to realisable goals.

6. A broad range of key people was identified and encouraged to take initiatives at their various levels. This meant that after the initial spear-head made by the HMI, progress was made on a broad front.

7. While it was accepted that time was needed for such a fundamental change, planning was systematic but not prolonged. Consequently, the initial impetus was maintained and events moved quickly enough to provide the schools, colleges and education authorities concerned with a sense of achievement.

8. The collaborative nature of the whole exercise and the establishment of joint planning committees involving school, college and education authority personnel meant that it was possible to meet the need for enhanced professional competence at teacher level and at the same time take into account the needs of schools and pupils as seen by school and education authority management.

9. Education authorities established a real partnership with the training institutions and many of the traditional barriers between 'town' and 'gown' simply disappeared.

This case study has presented a national policy and a strategy for development which embodies certain principles which seems to be gaining general acceptance in Scotland at least. Perhaps the general adoption of this kind of framework means we are simply looking at 'a set of ideas' about staff development 'whose time has come'. But it would be gratifying to think, for once, that the model of staff development generated by the Progress Report has had a definitive effect in the wider context of mainstream education.

Chapter Thirteen

THE CHALLENGE OF MICRO-TECHNOLOGY

Tim Southgate

During the past few years there has been considerable interest in the educational applications of micro-technology. Probably nowhere has this interest been greater than in the area of special educational needs, and as a result of government schemes or individual effort, large amounts of computer hardware have appeared in special schools. A survey of two education authorities early in 1984 revealed that over sixty per cent of special schools already had at least one computer (Fuller and Southgate, 1984). Many teachers in special classes and units are now giving a high priority to making this technology available to their pupils.

This enthusiastic response to the microcomputer in education has taken place alongside moves to develop the curriculum in special schools. Staff have felt themselves under pressure from advisers, inspectors and administrators, to improve their curricula; there has been an emphasis on the need for special schools to have much clearer aims and objectives. Although many schools are still in the early stages of this process, it would seem appropriate for the introduction of such a flexible and powerful new technology, which may have considerable implications for the curriculum and the whole teaching approach, to serve the aims and objectives of the school. Surprisingly, there has been little apparent connection between the curriculum development process and the acquisition and use of computers in the classroom.

In part, this rather ad hoc introduction of the computer into special schools could itself be seen as a consequence of not having clear aims and objectives. Green et al., (1982) make the point that the absence of any secure curriculum framework has resulted in special education becoming unusually susceptible to ideas and methods which have been grasped with enthusiasm but are seen as panaceas. However, the lack of a close connection between the development of curriculum aims and objectives and the use

161

of computers is also partly due to the different origins of these two movements. Pressure to improve and develop the curriculum has come in the main from above and outside the school. It is due as much to the need to justify the cost of special schools, at a time when the movement towards integration is challenging their existence, as it is to any desire to improve the quality of the education offered within them. The enthusiasm for microcomputers on the other hand has stemmed largely from the grass roots. It has grown as a result of teachers individually and in groups trying out the technology and passing on the promising outcomes of their experiences to others. This distinction is perhaps demonstrated by the way in which in-service courses dealing with curriculum planning are frequently initiated and led by administrators, advisers, inspectors or college lecturers, while those concerned with micro-technology usually have a much stronger input from teachers and therapists who are working directly with children.

Why is there such strong interest in the use of computers in special education? In the past there have been many new waves of interest in education and some of these were received with an enthusiasm at least equal to that now greeting micro-technology. Often these waves receded again almost as quickly as they came, leaving only a flotsam of expensive equipment or materials as evidence of their passing. However, micro-electronic circuits are becoming more and more powerful and at the same time less expensive. It is certain, therefore, that the application of micro-technology will continue to permeate into more and more areas of our lives, and for this reason alone, it would seem appropriate that all children should at least become familiar with computers.

The Computer as Instructor

However, there is more to the enthusiasm for computers than a desire to ensure that children are familiar with them as part of their preparation for life. From the earliest days teachers began to report that their children showed markedly more concentration, and for much longer periods, when working with the computer. Since motivation is a major concern of special needs teachers, many have welcomed the computer as a means of giving practice in specific skills.

One headteacher enthused over a program which had been written for him by a friend and was intended to 'teach deaf children to spell'. A word was displayed on the screen for a few seconds after which it disappeared. The child was then asked to reproduce the word. If it was not spelt correctly the computer burped and a sad face appeared followed by a cross. A correct spelling was rewarded by a small tick and the next word was then displayed. The only control the teacher had over the program was to select the 'level of difficulty' at the beginning. Of course, whatever it was doing, this program was certainly not teaching spelling and yet, such is the faith in the power of this technology, that the head concerned was prepared to suspend completely his normal judgement of what constituted sound educational material. Unfortunately, this view of the computer as a sort of ever-patient classroom assistant providing endless 'drill and practice' is very limiting. It taps only a fraction of the computer's potential and, according to a study reported in Goldenberg (1984), achieves no more than a narrow competence in that which is being practised. Narrow, sterile skill-getting will remain precisely that, whether transmitted by microcomputer or not (Green et. al,).

Sadly, the emphasis given to the need for behavioural objectives by many of the advocates of curriculum planning may have encouraged the instructional use of the computer. In addition, the difficulty of 'persuading established teachers to change their teaching approach for more than a few weeks or months' (Hammond, 1983) and a lack of adequate training has meant that many teachers employ computers in a way which supports and reinforces the existing approach. Certainly, most of the programs now in use in schools employ a 'didactic, question-answer, stimulus-response approach' (Green et. al, 1982). Most of these programs do not know what they are doing, i.e., they do not know enough about the subject under discussion, in the sense of being able to answer unanticipated questions, and they do not know enough about an individual student to be able to adapt the teaching session to his needs (O'Shea and Self, 1983).

Discovery Learning and the Computer

Fortunately, the potential contribution of the computer in special education is not limited to providing drill and practice and arid instruction. The 'instructional' role is only one of several distinguished for the computer by Odor (1984). When the computer is given a 'revelatory role', learning is by discovery. The subject matter is revealed to the children individually or in groups as they interact with a game, model, or simulation. Games and models are, of course, a well established means of imparting knowledge. Most infants have their classroom 'shop' and play 'word bingo'. Reading scheme teachers' manuals, such as that for the series '1-2-3 and Away' (McCullough, 1972) often contain numerous ideas for games intended to reinforce the scheme's vocabulary. Some teachers have recreated models of the 'Village with Three

Corners' in their classrooms and encourage the children to act out scenes from the stories.

While classroom games can be both motivating and effective in 'revealing' knowledge to the learner, the interaction with a computer can often involve the child even more and, as a result, be more effective. No one can doubt the motivational power of computer games. Many commercial 'adventure game' programs are available while some of those written for educational use have 'handlers' which enable the teacher to modify the content to suit different levels of ability.

Many programs employing computer models have been produced for children with special needs. At a very early level, the child may interact with the computer by pressing a switch or switches to achieve some result on the screen. For example, in one program, the child operates a switch to cause a horse to move across the screen. When the horse reaches a fence, another switch must be pressed before it will jump and then the first switch again to make it continue. More advanced is the program Podd (Acorn, 1984). Podd is an indeterminate creature with a large, round, red face. At the top of the screen the words 'Podd can' appear and the children have to guess what Podd can do. Language use, not spelling, is the aim so the teacher types in the children's suggestions and Podd then performs. 'He' can fly, run, sleep and do lots of other things and if he can't do a particular action he says so.

One of the programs in the Microspecial Pack (SMDP, 1984), which was designed for use by children aged fourteen to sixteen who have moderate learning difficulties, simulates a bank. Each pupil has a personal bank account and can deposit and withdraw amounts of his or her own choosing. The program includes a simulation of a 'cashcard' type till and, by pressing areas of an overlay keyboard and typing in a personal number, the pupil can withdraw money, find out how much is in the account, or request a bank statement.

The 'revelatory' role of the computer is an attractive alternative to its use as an instructor. It permits a variety of teaching styles and can be used with individuals and groups. It particularly fits well with the special education philosophy of assessing children by their performance at a task rather than by some norm-related score. The scope for individualisation remains quite limited. In the banking program, the teacher is able to alter the name of the bank and the colour schemes of the cheques on the screen but little else. The actions Podd can perform are fixed within the program. Even where the teacher does have more control over the content and level of the program, the curriculum content remains relatively fixed and the computer is still being used to reinforce the existing approach.

It is not impossible that it is this existing approach which is limiting the child's performance. The Warnock Report (1978) suggested that there are perhaps twenty per cent of children who will have special educational needs at some time in their school careers. This figure has been taken on board by heads and advisers to support demands for additional resources and increased special needs provision. If the twenty per cent do exist is it perhaps partly due to the way schools are organised and run? If children were not labelled as failures from an early stage by streaming, by putting them into CSE rather than GCE groups, by labelling them non-examination children, or by eventually ejecting them, is it possible that a smaller proportion of children would have special educational needs?

The Child in Control

Most existing approaches to the education of children with special needs leave the child with little control over his learning. This is particularly so with the 'developmental' curricula applied in many schools for children with severe learning handicaps. Even in the 'life skills' programs designed to make children with moderate learning difficulties more independent, the task and level of performance is often outside the pupil's control. Papert (1980) maintains that, by using the computer in a way which gives the child control, learning will be enormously enhanced. Papert with others devised a computer programming language called Logo specifically to enable children to have this control. The most well-known application of Logo is its use to construct shapes either on the computer screen or on the floor using a Turtle. The child enters a series of instructions in order to make the computer construct a shape. This shape may be determined in advance by the child or he may evolve it as the program progresses. There is therefore no right or wrong result and mistakes can easily be erased or utilised to make a new shape. Children using Logo alone or as part of a team experience not only control but also problem solving and decision making. The level at which it is used is determined by the learner not the teacher and, as the children learn by doing, the gains can be seen in understanding and in confidence. Papert even suggests that by using the computer in this 'conjectural' role children can come to understand abstract concepts earlier than the 'Piagetian' stages of development might suggest is possible. It is certainly possible that some of the barriers to learning encountered by special needs children could be broken down.

The Emancipation of the Learner

One of the main barriers to learning encountered by children with special needs is that to practise a particular skill the learner often has to perform many other operations as well. In order to develop creative writing ability, for instance, the child must hold a pen, be able to form letters correctly, and usually spell as well as think about the content and structure that is to be written. It is perhaps not surprising that poor motivation results from unsuccessful attempts to combine all these skills. For some children, severely impaired motor functioning or sensory loss may constitute an almost insurmountable barrier to the development of other skills. Recent experience has clearly demonstrated how the micro-computer can play an emancipatory role and remove or alleviate performance blocks in one area which are interfering with learning in another (Odor, 1984).

In the past few years a wide range of special devices has been developed to help overcome the communication and learning difficulties of children with physical or sensory impairments. Special switches and keyboards have been devised to exploit very limited movement or control. These new micro-electronic aids have the advantage of being much lighter, quieter, more reliable and less expensive than the mechanical devices which preceded them.

The real power and flexibility of the computer is in the software. The MAC-Apple program is perhaps one of the best examples of software designed to improve the communication of people with severe physical impairments (Poon, 1981). The MAC-Apple is a word-processor program. It can be operated by one switch or two switches, an eight-way switch, or through a normal or modified keyboard and can be completely 'personalised' to the abilities of the user. Text can be entered a letter at a time or in whole words or phrases which, of course, increases speed of output while reducing effort. The text can be corrected or edited before being printed out or stored on disc.

Sandy is a severely physically and speech impaired girl of fifteen who is only able to be integrated into an ordinary comprehensive school because she has a MAC-Apple system. Her Apple computer is mounted on a trolley and moved around the building. Sandy stores her work on a disc and, as she has another system at home, this is usually all she has to take home in the evening to do her homework.

The use of special word processor programs can emancipate children with a wide range of special needs. The WRITE program is an example of the way in which the computer can be used to focus on individual areas of skill (Fuller et. al, 1983). In this program the child writes on the screen in large letters. This may be free or copy writing. When a word is completed the space bar is pressed and the word drops to the bottom half of the screen where a sentence is built up. When copying from the 'teacher's' line, the child may be guided as to which is the next letter by a small underlining cursor. If the teacher finds that this is not necessary or a distraction it can be removed or replaced by a synthesised voice. The use of speech synthesis in this way can reinforce the child's own language and be particularly effective. It is also a valuable feature which enables the program to be used by visually impaired children.

Clearly these different roles for the computer in education overlap and it is not difficult to find programs with the features of more than one role. In many instances the role the computer fulfils will depend not on the software but on how the system is used. Odor distinguishes the 'computer as teacher' and the 'computer as tool'. It is to be hoped that what has been said demonstrates that the computer is not a very effective teacher. Some hold the view that computers will one day be so powerful and the science of artificial intelligence so developed that the human teacher can be replaced. This seems an unlikely eventuality and the view probably reveals more about the holder's model of learning and teachers than any ability to prophesy. It is also to be hoped that what has been said demonstrates that the computer is, for the teacher, a very powerful and flexible 'tool, though not the only one to promote learning for students whose needs are not being met' (Goldenberg et. al, 1984).

The Need for Training

Using any tool effectively requires training and practice. The computer, because of its enormous versatility, requires probably more experience than other tools that are available to the teacher. In more than one education authority teachers used to be required successfully to complete a course of instruction before they were permitted to handle audio-visual equipment. It is not uncommon to find computers being unpacked and introduced into the classroom by teachers who have little or no training.

In the schools included in the survey described earlier (Fuller and Southgate, 1984) few members of staff had had more than very basic computer familiarisation. Most of their knowledge was self-gained and supplemented by visits to other schools or to one of the four Special Education Micro-electronics Resource Centres (SEMERCS). Hammond (1983)

maintained that in the United States teachers in middle and
senior schools receive only fifteen minutes training before
they begin to use microcomputers in the classroom. It is
perhaps not surprising that as a result they tend to use the
machine in a limited instructional way.

What Sort of Training is Needed?

ACSET recommended that there should be a special education
element in the initial training of all teachers. Special
needs is such a complex area that to make such an element more
than a quick sketch of the problems and possible responses
will require the commitment of a considerable amount of time
and other resources. At present most colleges have done
little more than begin to make their students aware of the
educational possibilities of micro-technology. To expect the
development in the near future of any meaningful component of
initial training which combines both special needs and
micro-technology is therefore unrealistic. The majority of
teacher education in this field will continue to be, and is
probably best, undertaken through in-service courses.

Where the emphasis will lie in these courses will
probably change with time. The earliest courses organised
were heavily biased towards familiarity with the hardware.
Much time was spent unpacking, connecting up, and learning to
load programs (usually from cassettes). But knowing how to
operate a film projector does not ensure that you will show
educationally useful films and knowing how to operate a
computer is no guarantee that it will be used properly. It is
possible that a course which concentrates on the mechanics
will tend to reinforce a mechanistic view of learning. The
next generation of teachers will come from a more computerate
generation and there will be less of the technophobia of today
to overcome. Hopefully the emphasis will change from hardware
to software.

A manual for an ILEA Pilot Project In-service training
course on Computers in Special Education devotes much of its
space to how to load, run and copy programs. The remainder is
given over to the handling of programs in BASIC. The question
of whether teachers should produce educational software has
often been discussed. It cannot be dismissed with the
argument that teachers don't write books so why should they
write programs. There are thousands of excellent educational
books from which to choose. In one school in the survey
mentioned earlier the head claimed that all the staff had
learnt to program in BASIC because they had been unable to
find any software that suited their needs.

Writing good special educational software takes a great deal of skill, sensitivity and time. In spite of thousands of man-hours invested in this task over the past few years there have been to date very few worthwhile programs included. There is nothing wrong at all with teachers learning to program computers in BASIC or any other language. The best use for this skill is communicating software specifications to programmers and making minor modifications to existing programs. Time spent on writing programs would be better spent on preparation and relaxation.

In spite of the present dearth of good software it is probable that in the near future much more advanced authoring systems will be developed which will enable teachers to develop their own materials with little effort. The ability to program will become as unnecessary as the ability to create fire without matches.

What then should be the aims of future in-service training for teachers using micro-technology with special needs children? If teachers will not require technical knowledge or the ability to write programs what will they need? One head summed up the need in his school as knowing how to tie it in to the curriculum. Clearly if a school has developed its curriculum after much careful consideration it would be reasonable for the computer work to adopt a broadly similar style and serve similar objectives. It would, for instance, be hard to justify using the computer in an entirely instructional role when the school curriculum is based on discovery learning.

In order to tie the computer into the curriculum teachers first need not only to be aware of the aims and objectives of the curriculum they are following but also appreciate the learning model upon which it is based. They will then need to become aware of the strengths and limitations of micro-computers as a learning resource (Green et. al, 1982). Probably the main source of information on micro-technology and special education has been the Special Education Micro-electronic Resources Centres mentioned above. Four SEMERCs were established, in London, Newcastle, Manchester and Bristol, as part of the government's Micro-electronics Education Project (MEP). Additional resources have now been provided to enable the SEMERCs to increase their in-service training contribution and also to establish the ACE Centre at Ormerod School in Oxford. This Centre will provide information and advice on the use of micro-electronic communication aids in education.

This kind of in-service training is not very different from that already provided in other areas. Courses are offered on how to use various media such as slides and video to enhance the existing curriculum and workshops are organised to share experiences of applying particular approaches to teaching a particular subject. This sort of in-service training also supports the notion of using the computer to reinforce existing approaches. The computer is such a powerful tool that it permits us to think beyond the existing curriculum and beyond the limitations we perceive to a child's thinking and learning. It permits us to explore what happens when the unproductive workload of the child or teacher is reduced and the child himself takes greater control of a small part of his learning.

Exactly how in-service training can help foster this use of the computer remains to be seen. Clearly teachers need to be aware of the emancipatory contribution the computer can make. They need also an awareness of the possibilities for a different type of learning that are opened up by Logo and the Turtle. Perhaps most of all, if the child with special needs is to have greater control over his learning, then the teacher, so accustomed to being in control of everything in the classroom, will have to learn to relinquish some of that control.

Conclusions

Computer technology is here to stay both in our lives and in our schools and technology has enormous implications for the education of children with special needs. Computers have been widely used in an instructional role but in this role they reinforce the most arid of existing approaches. The computer is not a teacher and we should not try to use it as such. Instead the computer is a powerful and flexible tool which can uniquely enhance the learning of children with special needs. It can be used very effectively to encourage learning by discovery. More exciting is the way the computer can emancipate the learner by augmenting communication, reducing blocks to learning, and give him control over his learning. Teachers need in-service training to help align computer use with the existing curriculum. However, if the full potential of the computer for special children is to be realised, teachers will also need to learn how to relinquish some of their control and join the child in learning.

Chapter Fourteen

IN-SERVICE TRAINING AT THE OPEN UNIVERSITY - A NON-SELECTIVE
APPROACH TO SPECIAL NEEDS?

Tony Booth

Introduction

Every institution embodies a set of contradictions which
are partly established by its history but are also a simple
reflection of contradictions within society.   If the Open
University were to be a truly non-selective institution it
would cease to qualify as a university.   Equally there is
something wrong about the giving of extra credentials to
teachers in order to enable them to place equal value on their
pupils irrespective of their ability or disability.   And I do
not think that this is a trivial point serving only as an
opportunity for self-criticism.   For it seems possible to me
that the professionalisation of knowledge by teachers and
others is a root cause of the learning difficulties of pupils.

The creators of any course need to ask themselves: will
the experience of the course reduce or expand the knowledge of
the participants? Will the course dissipate or concentrate the
energy of its members? Is there another activity in which the
participants could engage which might be of greater benefit to
their practice? We need to be open about the events within our
own experience which enable us to reflect on and change our
practice and also to recognise that different people may think
and adapt in different styles.   The course itself must conform
to a theory of education, consciously adopted. Should it be an
aim of all courses to enable students to become aware of and
develop their own interests as well as reasons and motives for
action?   There is a second related contradiction involved in
producing courses on 'Special Needs in Education': even those
which espouse a coherent philosophy of integration.   Not only
may they perpetuate separate courses for 'special' and 'non

special' teachers, but for colleagues and others not participating in the course, their very existence may perpetuate a view of separate special education held by these non-participants.

A half-credit course; 'Special Needs in Education'

If a course is to be relevant to the needs of teachers it has to respond to their existing conceptions of the issues, the practice within their schools and local education authorities, as well as current national policies. Our existing half-credit course 'Special Needs in Education', which in its first four years since 1982 will have been taken by about 3,200 students, attempts to provide a thorough description and analysis of current theory and practice in 'special education'. When we were planning the course we became aware that there was no detailed description of the range of practices and provision labelled as 'special' in the United Kingdom. In depicting special education, authors tended to outline a view of good practice as if it could be found generally in schools and many texts were heavily prescriptive. However, the value of prescriptions about *future* practice must depend on a thorough knowledge of *existing* practice. The reality of schools and classrooms is rarely portrayed and that is something we tried to do in the first half of our course and in particular by supporting text and radio and television programmes with case-study material (Booth and Statham, 1982) as well as more conventional articles (Swann, 1982).

It has become commonplace to describe schools as having both an official and hidden curriculum. However that schools select and stratify pupils in preparation for the labour market in terms of their 'ability', class, sex and colour can hardly any longer be regarded as a secret of schooling. But we can also identify a hidden-hidden curriculum in schools, comprising issues which can dominate school life but which are more rarely discussed; the understandable preoccupation with classroom control, the career aspirations of teachers, conflicts amongst staff, the extent to which schools provide a social arena for both staff and pupils. An understanding of this hidden-hidden curriculum, that pupils and teachers are ordinary people like the rest of us, is an essential prerequisite to any strategy for real change in schools.

This everyday knowledge of schooling is also the most important source of information about what schools are like and is one of the means by which students can participate in the development of the 'knowledge' within a course. By not only valuing the experience and knowledge they already possess but by also regarding it as an essential feature of their assignments we have tried to avoid the paradox which afflicts students on many courses. Their own experience may be treated as mere anecdotes, irrelevant to the 'real' knowledge contained in the course. Yet when the course is finished students are expected to insert this esoteric knowledge into their day to day practice. Whilst the course is studied at a distance, then, we have tried to make the experience of studying it as immediate as possible.

We have attempted to be honest with ourselves about what can be achieved by distance-learning on a course open to both teachers and non-teachers and to make this variety of student perspectives a strength of the course. Some LEAs through the use of block-bookings have formed groups of teachers for whom it is possible to link the course to a local development plan. But we reject the distinctions between practical and theoretical or skills-based and knowledge-based courses. We see the course as enabling teacher-students to reflect on and revise their practices and this appears to be the way students see it themselves. Within its teacher-students the course includes people working in primary, secondary and nursery schools as well as special schools, though there is an emphasis on the 5-16 age range. It is a generic course, covering the education of pupils with disabilities and the wider issues of the production and reduction of failure and disaffection in schools. These concerns are linked by their perception as part of 'special education' and by their common inclusion in the activities of certain professional groups. However, the creation of special education also depends on answers to the question 'Who is normal in our schools?' It is intimately associated with the valuation and devaluation of pupils in terms of their competence, attainments and appearance. The course involves a *critical* account of 'special education' but it would appear strange to us for a university to attempt anything other than a searching analysis.

Open University courses are studied throughout Great Britain and Northern Ireland and in reflecting practice and possibility we tried to draw on material throughout the U.K. This has created problems in terminology and relevance. In Scotland I am informed there is now no 'special education'. In Northern Ireland some pupils are still defined as ineducable and secondary education is selective. The term 'integration' refers there to catholics and protestants sharing schooling.

In planning the course content we adhered loosely to a progression through three questions: what is going on in 'special education'; how do we make sense of what goes on; how can we improve what goes on? As will be clear from a later chapter, the answer to the last question is not taken to be unproblematic.   The first half of the course is devoted, largely, to a portrayal of the current state of special education in the United Kingdom, the effect on pupils and their families, prospects for further education and employment, the nature of 'special' curricula, the development and involvement of professionals and the management and control of the 'special education system' (Swann, Booth and Potts, 1982).

In the second half of the course we have moved on from an examination of what is happening in the United Kingdom in order to acquire a deeper perspective on current practice and to develop constructive alternatives.   We have looked at the historical roots of special education in the development of popular education and at comparisons with other developed nations: examined attempts made to account for children's difficulties in biological, psychological, sociological and political terms: analysed the relationships between research, practice and progress in special education: and looked at the scope for preventing handicaps and educational difficulties. Finally, in Unit 16, we attempted to draw the course together by presenting a number of practical suggestions for the formation of an education system in which almost all children participate in the social and educational life of ordinary 'comprehensive' primary and secondary schools (Booth, Potts and Swann, 1983).

In defining our terms we have adhered to ordinary language as closely as possible. As far as I can see the most sensible way of defining special needs is as 'unmet needs'. When they are met they cease to exist. Children have special needs, then, when they have needs and interests to which their schools do not currently respond. We have not dispensed with the use of 'handicap' but have given it its traditional meaning instead. A handicap is a burden or disadvantage and can be the result of physical impairmant but may also arise from social or economic inequalities.   Children have learning difficulties when they find something, *some particular thing,* difficult to learn.   They arise from a mismatch between what someone is trying to do or being asked or expected to do and what they are currently able to do. Learning difficulties do not define a category of children but a relationship between people and tasks.

Integration forms a major theme of the course and is introduced and discussed from the beginning. The integration debate is of central significance because it involves a set of ideas which can form the basis of a philosophy for special education not just because it is currently controversial.   An integration principle also happens to have been espoused in official government documents since the early-fifties. At the planning stage of the course we agreed on this principle that 'wherever possible pupils with disabilities or who experience difficulties should be included in ordinary schools'. But it was clear that the adoption of an integration principle involved a commitment to a change in practice; to a desire to see pupils from the special school sector within ordinary schools wherever this could be made possible. We attempted, then, to close the gap between official rhetoric and practical commitment (Booth, 1981).

But integration cannot be defined sensibly, only in terms of the inclusion of pupils and the resources they require in ordinary schools from the special school sector. By the end of the course the idea of integration in education has been extended to become the process of increasing the participation of all members of the communities of ordinary schools in the social and educational life within them. This covers children and adults with disabilities, and also all pupils, parents and other community members whose participation could be enhanced. The process of integration merges then into the creation of comprehensive community education in nursery, primary and secondary schools. This process itself involves a transfer of power from included to excluded groups: it is essentially a political process.

Integration and the creation of comprehensive community education are both intimately concerned with the way normality is defined in schools and to fostering the notion that normality includes or even celebrates difference. They are concerned with the creation of an education system in which the value ascribed to pupils is not dependent on their sex, class, ethnic backkground, family structure, ability or disability. Initiatives in special education merge then with other community initiatives such as those to combat sexism and racism in schooling. It shares with such initiatives a dependence on two fundamental questions. Who do the overt and hidden curricula of a school include and exclude? How can the curricula of a school reflect the sex, interests, family structure, backgrounds, cultures and capacities of its members and value them all? A black girl finding difficulty in reading a history book emphasising white male culture requires one kind of curriculum adaptation not three.

By the end of the half-credit course students are expected to be able to devise plans for an integrated system in the context of comprehensive community education. In extending this first course into an advanced diploma and in creating a short in-service course we intend to look in detail at the curriculum content, teaching methods and forms of organisation and finance that can support such a system.

175

The Advanced Diploma

The content of our advanced diploma has been partly determined by what was omitted from our earlier course but its form is heavily influenced by the availability of funds. The structure is shown in Appendix 1 Part One consists of Special Needs in Education, Part Two consists of a compatible half-credit education or social science course and Part Three consists of a full - credit project course based around three new externally published text-books which are being written specifically for the course. This new material represents our attempt to set the issues of special education firmly within the context of ideas about mainstream curricula. We do not see special educators as technologists, offering the means by which existing curricula can be adapted to the 'level' of the learner or to the disability of pupils. We see them as intimately concerned with understanding, challenging and devising curriculum content.

A short course - The prevention of learning difficulties

The first module of the project year, 'Curricula for All', is being linked to a short 20 session course and at some future date we hope to do the same with the other modules. I will discuss the content of this course in some detail in order to give a clearer idea of the way we are attempting to reconnect remedial and special education within the mainstream, and revise the conceptions of specialists that this entails. The headings for the 20 sessions of the course are shown in Appendix 1. The impetus for this work arose from a request from the Grampian region that we create an in-service course for them to assist their attempts to reshape their approach to remedial education. But the issues raised are quite general and we are currently preparing this material as a national short course.

At the same time as the Warnock report was prepared and published (DES, 1978) the Scottish HMI produced a slim document entitled 'The Education of Pupils with Learning Difficulties; a progress report by HM inspectors of schools' (SED, 1978). It could be argued that the positive efffects on practice of the two reports have been in inverse proportion to their size.

The Scottish report placed the major responsibility for the creation of learning difficulties on the narrow focus and method of presentation of the curriculum in schools. It gave remedial education a broad definition, arguing that up to fifty per cent of the school population could experience learning difficulties. It suggested that rather than provide a casualty service for school failures remedial specialists should have a

176

direct and officially sanctioned role in supporting class and subject teachers to develop differentiated curricula through planning, consultation and cooperative teaching. The report stressed this shift in approach arguing that 'appropriate, rather than remedial, education is required'. Mixed-ability learning and teaching were to be extended and the withdrawal of pupils kept to a minimum. Special attention was to be paid to transfer between primary and secondary school. A principal remedial education teacher with the same status as heads of subject departments was to have special responsibility for tackling learning difficulties in comprehensive schools and an assistant head teacher was to have this role in primary schools. Whilst the remedial specialists were to have a special role in fostering cooperative teaching and curriculum development, the head teacher was to ensure that all staff took responsibility for dealing with the learning difficulties experienced by pupils in their classes.

All advisory staff were to recognise 'remedial education' as an essential part of their work. Finally, each LEA was to designate a senior coordinator to foster these policies and ensure that remedial staff were distributed according to need. Whilst the document has been interpreted in different ways and implemented to varying extents by different Scottish LEAs, the surprising result was that all LEAs have taken them up in some way and some, Fife and Grampian for example, have elaborated them into a region-wide policy. In Grampian they have introduced remedial teams into a sector of schools consisting of a comprehensive school and its feeder primaries in most areas of the region. The team is led by a principal remedial teacher in the secondary schools. The HMI report had stressed the difference between remedial provision for primary and secondary schools arguing that 'the role of consultant to subject specialists in secondary schools makes training for that sector quite different from that for primary schools'. In Grampian, however, they introduced 'float teachers' to work in both primary and secondary schools.

The Scottish HMI report recommended training in remedial education for all teachers as well as specialist training courses. National guidelines for new training courses have been devised and the colleges of education have produced a new *Diploma in Learning Difficulties* now referred to as the Diploma in Special Educational Needs (non-recorded pupils). This Diploma inculcates the four new roles of Scottish remedial teachers: consultancy, cooperative teaching, direct tuition for *persistent* difficulties in basic reading and number and support for pupils with temporary learning or emotional difficulties.

Whilst our in-service course is related to the new

directions in remedial education taking place in Scotland it is not bound by conceptions of the issues there. The Scottish changes are based on an attempt to revise the boundaries between remedial and special education and echo the slogan issuing from Coventry 'every teacher is a teacher of special needs'. But the distinction between pupils requiring ordinary and specialist education are retained in Scottish training with separate diplomas on learning difficulties and 'severe and complex' special needs. This may exacerbate problems of integration especially where groups of children with disabilities are in ordinary schools and two separately trained support services operate side by side. The existence of different primary and secondary diplomas has made it difficult to offer training to 'float' teachers in Grampian.

Our course takes seriously the injunction to remove the boundaries between 'remedial', 'special' and 'ordinary' education. It is intended for *all* teachers and is designed so that the activity of working on it also involves its partial implementation. It can be used by LEAs to form the basis of a policy for special needs. It is intended for joint study by a group of support teachers and class and subject teachers drawn from a sector of schools; a secondary and its feeder primaries. It would make sense for representatives of any special school whose pupils are drawn from these schools and who could be supported back within them to be attached to this group too. If cooperative teaching and planning between support teachers and others are to become a reality then teachers need to share a common language and jointly devise policies for their schools. It is essential therefore that they should share in in-service training.

As teachers share their knowledge and expertise and accept a more generic rôle in secondary as well as primary schools, 'every teacher a teacher of science' may become as relevant a slogan as 'every teacher a teacher of special needs'.

The opening session of the course is devoted to creating a common language for course participants, putting common sense into the language of special education and in understanding difficulties in learning as a breakdown in the relationship between pupils and curricula. We will talk of curriculum support teachers rather than remedial or specialist teachers. We will examine the meaning of a whole school policy in the context of a reality of conflict within many schools on both major and minor issues.

Since we see a programme for special needs as part of a single scheme for adapting curricula for all we regard the attempt to relate the curriculum to the capacities, backgrounds and interests of all pupils, to reflect pupils in curricula, as a more fundamental and inclusive exercise than finding pupils who cannot cope with the level of language or concept in the classroom. We need to ask whom does the curriculum include and exclude? It is only after the experience and abilities of all pupils are valued that the appropriate *level* of learning and teaching can be understood. Further, as we allow the experience and abilities of pupils to determine the curriculum we move away from a predetermined curriculum based on teacher produced materials and worksheets.

We are examining a variety of case studies of curriculum adaptation. The 'Tour de France' scheme adopted in some Scottish schools, although it has been criticised for its reliance on predetermined behavioural objectives, is an attempt to incorporate all levels of ability in learning French, an area where our xenophobic attitudes and views about ability have combined to deprive remedial and special children from learning a second language. Primary science schemes will be analysed both in terms of the extent to which they permit all pupils access to them and by the relevance of their content to the experience of pupils. Asking questions about the world within your experience and thereby extending your experience of the world is the foundation of science and ... perhaps education.

We will consider the diverse ways in which the relationship between curriculum and community is interpreted. Commonly, community-involvement means parent-involvement or more specifically *mothers* reading with their children at home. We will look at such schemes as they have operated for example in Haringey (Times Educational Supplement, 11/3/83, p.20). But we will also examine ways of including the community in the centre of the curriculum in work such as the Arbury project; a mixed ability oral history project in a working-class area of Cambridge, or the Vauxhall Manor Drama Project - Motherland.

This process of analysing curricula, both official and hidden, and matching them to pupils supercedes traditional approaches to screening and diagnosing children. The use of screening tests for measuring pupils skills which are unrelated to either the curriculum of a particular school or the background and interests of particular pupil is counterproductive. It re-introduces a defect model and discourages the rethinking of the nature of special needs in pupils. The same applies to the use of diagnostic tests which connect to a special curriculum in subskills of basic skills unrelated to interest and experience of pupils - and encourages withdrawal teaching and labelling of pupils as slow learners.

179

After exploring the notion of community-centred project based curricula within groups mixed in ability, interest, sex and background we will look more specifically at the involvement of support teachers. The development of team teaching between support and class and subject teachers has been a cornerstone of developments in Scotland and has been implemented across the curriculum with varying results. I see the introduction of cooperative teaching as a powerful method for analysing, revising and adapting curricula and for moving away from traditional teaching rôles. But if cooperative teaching is tied to the notion of remedial education its introduction has dangers. For it could also become a powerful way of inculcating an inappropriate ideology about pupils with special needs into every classroom.

Cooperative teaching between support teachers and others has to be seen as part of the process of spreading expertise which will result in a re-evaluation of specialism and offers an excellent opportunity to bring some important issues out into the open. Whatever training teachers have had it will always be true that the skills and experience they have to offer are the skills and experience they actually possess not ones we expect them to have as a result of their status, salary and credentials. A science specialist may actually have had considerable experience in adapting materials to reduce difficulties in learning and a remedial specialist may have been a science teacher.

Rather than thinking of the essence of support teaching as residing in knowledge and skills in relation to categories of children it may be better to think of it as particular rôles for supporting and enhancing differentiated teaching and learning. One of the new roles of specialists in learning difficulties which has caused much debate in Scotland is the notion of consultancy. It has been taken to imply the possession of expertise on the process of learning, the analysis of curriculum materials and their adaptation as well as the management of professional relationships. We have emphasised the activity rather than any special expertise on which it may depend by talking of *consulting* (and *coordinating*) rather than *consultancy*, with the expectation of the flow of expertise being two-way.

Another rôle which has emerged in practice, though is not present in the official view in Scotland, is that of managing centralised resources within a school and this highlights a further danger of the developments I am discussing. For there is a tendency to think of the implementation of curricula adapted to pupils as involving a mass of prepackaged materials or worksheets prepared for three curriculum levels in the mixed ability group. This tendency may be enhanced where support teachers begin to get involved in a content area rather than with pupils. To what extent then should the notion of minimum withdrawal of pupils imply a minimum centralisation of curriculum materials?

We have attempted to re-analyse the notion of withdrawal partly by re-labelling it tutorial time! Just as we would wish to challenge the assumption that specialist teaching should take place outside the classroom we would not wish to introduce a new sanctity of the class group with one teacher. In fact it is a useful exercise to analyse the extent to which pupils are absent from a class group bearing in mind the wide possibilities for absence for illness, truancy, punishment, special duties, music, remedial help, counselling, medicals, community service, job interviews (Sayer, 1983).

The course goes on to consider the implications of the changes in approach we have been discussing for organising schools. We are using case studies to explore the effects of shrinking resources on the assessment of funding priorities. We hope to record discussions within a school about priority decisions and leave students within the course to come up with their own solutions for resolving competing interests.

We will be looking too, at possibilities for incorporating planning time into the school day and at methods for timetabling the human and physical resources of the school. We will also include a consideration of 16+ and other school assessments including profiles and the possible dangers of providing pupils with certificates of unemployability.

Concluding Remarks

In a previous chapter I argued that education is to be understood as an arena characterised by attempts to implement competing and conflicting philosophies. Special education or in-service training initiatives cannot be exempted from this reality and require careful attention to be paid to their underlying principles and general implications. In particular training initiatives must be understood in the context of other forces for change within education and in part they derive their meaning and effects from them.

I have tried to give some idea of an approach to training in special needs in education which is compatible with a comprehensive philosophy and which will enhance rather than undermine the development of comprehensive nursery, primary and secondary provision. The issues raised are inevitably broad and it is understandable that some teachers pine or cling onto the simplicity of solutions which allocate special pupils to

181

special schools and remedial pupils to remedial classes or broom cupboards where diagnostic tests can be administered, deficiencies discovered and a heavy dose of basic skills teaching can be prescribed and delivered. But unfortunately the simplicity or convenience of a solution to an educational problem is no guarantee of its efficacy *or* value. That is something which has to be assessed in terms of the extent to which it hinders or assists the implementation of a favoured educational philosophy. In the process of raising our underlying principles to consciousness we can make it more simple and natural to act upon them.

Of course a relocation of the problem of learning difficulties from inside the child or the child's background or culture or family to the curriculum in school cannot cause the problems within schools to evaporate, nor should it be seen as an attempt to hold teachers personally responsible for the difficulties which arise. Teachers are under massive pressures within a shrinking education system which is in turn adapting to shrinking employment opportunities for school leavers. There is a definite danger that a new focus on the curriculum within schools will deflect attention from the handicapping social conditions outside them or even hold schools responsible for such conditions. This is a clear strand in attempts to vocationalise the curriculum in secondary schools where high unemployment is blamed, in part, on the inappropriateness of the training given to the workforce which is offered vocational training after school and prevocational training within it. Schooling is not created anew by each generation of teachers and they operate within institutional constraints not of their choosing. The managerial functions of teachers, for example, may be in opposition to education, but they cannot be removed without a radical restructuring of schooling. Put at its simplest, pupils do not need education in the way they need food. By and large they are given schooling in the way they might be said to need a good dose of castor oil. Yet even if teachers work within circumstances which they do not select themselves the difficulties experienced by pupils are not totally beyond their control. Viewing difficulties in learning as arising from the relationship between pupils and curricula can enhance the contribution of teachers to their own working lives. But it can do so without imposing a new burden if it is recognised that the learning environments in which teachers are free to participate with pupils are severely constrained.

Chapter Fifteen

THE SILENT AGENDA OF SPECIAL EDUCATION

Neville Jones

The ACSET Agenda

Following the request of the Secretary of State for the Advisory Committee on the Supply and Education of Teachers (ACSET) to consider existing provision for the training of teachers of pupils in special schools and units, the special education content of general teacher training courses, and any implications for further education, the Report the Committee published in June 1984 was to a much wider remit. The Committee found the original brief far too narrow in scope: it had failed to take into account the changes in thinking and practice that had taken place in the last decade or more. The main changes are in the heightened awareness of the need to open up for the handicapped increased opportunities for access to a normal curriculum; a philosophic aim of normalisation; and the corollary of this, that such opportunities have to be sought in mainstream education.

The Warnock Report had broadened the field of special education beyond what was being provided in special schools: the figure of less than two per cent of school-age children in special schools was extended by the planning assumption that in the future a response would be required for about one in five children at some time during their school career. These children would be in ordinary schools. The 1981 Act had introduced a small element of legal jurisdiction, yet to be tested by case-law, but carrying the implication that there should be both an awareness and a response to children with special needs by all teachers who work in ordinary and special schools. The ACSET Working Group, therefore, refocused its thinking so that its recommendations would take into account and reflect, not only in principle but in specific proposals, both the training needs of teachers who would take specific responsibility for children with special needs in mainstream and special schools, and also the training required by *all* teachers in respect of special educational needs. Additional considerations were the educational needs of sixteen-to-nineteen-year-olds and the pre-school population aged two to five years.

By taking the initial brief to look at the training needs of teachers who would work in special schools and units, the ACSET Working Group could easily have confined its activities to clearing up some of the anomalies that existed in relation to teacher training and special education: in particular, the way that seven training courses currently equip teachers to take up immediate special responsibility posts in special schools without the teachers first having taught normal children. Clearly the circumstances which led to the 1970 Education Act required some emergency provision whereby the newly established schools for severely mentally handicapped children could be adequately staffed by qualified teachers. This need has now been met but teachers trained in this way are now having to face a career challenge arising from trends to integrate the severely mentally handicapped into ordinary schools. The additional expectation of these special educators is to work alongside ordinary teachers in educational contexts which are different to those for which they have been trained and where they have practical experience. Attempts are being made by these special teachers to work in ordinary schools in some style of 'consultancy' but the expertise required by teachers in ordinary schools is different to that required for teaching handicapped children in 'special' settings so this aim to provide such teachers with new roles in ordinary schools must be tempered with realism.

Moreover, while there is likely to be a decreasing demand for such specialist work, there is no evidence that, in spite of integration trends, the child populations of special schools are falling (Swann, 1985). What may be happening is that the children now being admitted are more handicapped, in a multiple sense, so this is an additional demand that pushes the special teacher even further away from normal school orientations. Caught in such professional dilemmas the ACSET Working Group was of the opinion that it was inappropriate for a group of teachers to find themselves competent in so limited a field of practice; hence the proposal that initial training courses designed principally for special education should be phased out and such training should be taken up only when teachers have qualified and become experienced in the teaching of normal children.

The Working Group made no recommendations on the question of salary enhancement for teachers who have acquired additional specialist qualifications, rightly arguing that this was a matter for the Burnham Committee. But it was an opportunity, and the right occasion, to set out the issues which the Burnham Committee in its wisdom could take into consideration.

Also the Working Group was not in a position to make firm proposals for teachers working with special educational and training needs in further education because of the novelty of much of the development in this area, but highlighted some areas where action might be taken. Clearly many of the issues discussed in relation to children aged five to sixteen appertain to further education, but central government interest and involvement in the fourteen-plus age group of students is now at high tide and an opportunity may well have been lost to build into further education ideas and planning that will take special needs forward into the next decade rather than just implant old special education orthodoxy. Already we see many further education establishments setting up courses for such groups as slow-learners because the FE model of courses, rather than subject based work, fit exactly the old DES system of categories for handicap. So we are witnessing the re-establishment of classified groups of handicapped students, for educational and training purposes, which only eight years ago the Warnock Report recommended we should abandon.

Towards a Future Agenda

The ACSET Working Group grasped very firmly, in spite of its obvious sensitivity, the question of the purpose, content, and tutor staffing of courses on special education. Special tutors face two immediate difficulties: how they relate and are supportive to other subject staff in their own institutions, and more broadly, how their courses can be integrated into the planning of overall activities of the teacher institution. The question here is not only about the availability of time but also of relevant expertise. Because historically special education refers to what happens in special schools, and more recently to what happens in segregated classes or special units in ordinary schools, there is an expectation that what will be taught will be the special education 'system'. This relates to teaching small groups of children with similar handicaps in separate accommodation and with what is called a special curriculum.

185

Hence many tutors are experts in this field, and courses draw heavily on school doctors, psychologists, special advisers, heads of special schools, to lecture and provide the didactic component. Practical work projects and theses are usually geared to some category of handicap and visits of observation are made to special schools. But the majority of teachers attending such courses teach in ordinary schools and will return to teach their ordinary classes. On the syllabus of many special courses, in-service and awareness courses, it is difficult to find the orientation that will help an ordinary teacher to know what to do in ordinary classes if they include children with special needs. These courses enjoy a measure of success only because what they provide for ordinary teachers is something novel and novelty engages interest.

What would be looked for in the future are courses planned for children's educational needs (not special education courses) by headteachers of ordinary schools or by ordinary teachers recognised as having a particular contribution to make. Lectures, seminars, visits, project work and theses would all fall into an integrated perspective as the focus for the courses would be towards ordinary schools and all the children who attend them.

Whatever changes the government decides to make in relation to the above issues, they well may be seen as a welcoming tidying up of arrangements, that in total do not affect substantially the system of education we call special. Any change might well reflect an attitude shift or a re-appraisal of priorities but underlying any discussion on special education are issues that seldom come on the agenda of any commission or working party or find expression in legislation. Too often the aim is to make some aspect of public provision a little more administratively tidy, to make adjustments for an anomaly here or a new demand over there, all of which are of immediate concern. Where, it might be asked, is the dialogue on where special education might be in, say, the year 2,000 or beyond? This is not to be dismissive of the critical literature of the last decade, or the attempts to denote the trends in ideological thinking and practice since public education developed its special characteristics.

The ACSET Committee had a specific task to perform, to make practical proposals that would facilitate developments according to a changing perspective of what special education could be about in the future. The Report may be said to have raised our sights a little, if only to draw attention to the fact that questions asked about special education are really

addressed to education in general. Of course, as long as
children are segregated in special provision then the
motivation for mainstream educators to make a response to
such questions is diminished.

We are aware of the actual agenda to which the members
of the ACSET Working Group gave their minds but it might be
of interest to speculate about the mental agenda of some of
its members, and others, that in the future might produce a
very different kind of report. Certainly on this silent
agenda would be issues like definition, dualism, and deficit
model education, all of which bedevil progress at the present
time in bringing together educational comprehensiveness for
the handicapped. This is not the place to explore these
areas in any depth but only to draw attention to some of the
parameters dilemmas.

Definitional problems are linked to questions about the
meaning of terms, and whatever are the confusions of defining
education in general, the term 'special education' is even more
evasive. The Oxford Dictionary of English Etymology defines
the word 'special' as 'exceeding what is usual or common'.
Does this mean we should refer to special teachers as
'uncommon teachers' or special schools as 'unusual schools'?
Clearly the language usage does not allow such freedom and we
are placed at even one more degree of abstraction because we
would want to define more precisely what is meant by being
'uncommon' and 'unusual'. If common means 'belonging equally
to two or more' then uncommon presumably means less than two
so that a special teacher becomes one of a kind. But
diversity in training, experience, and practice is the
characteristic among the group of teachers we call special,
and because many have never been trained or experienced in
teaching in ordinary schools the sense of unity, professional
or otherwise, becomes even less viable.

If usual means 'that which is in ordinary or common use'
then unusual presumably means that which is not ordinary or
common, and as we have discovered with defining the word
uncommon, we arrive at the stage of one kind of teacher and
one kind of special school. All we can conclude from this is
that a special teacher or school is one kind of teacher or
school which is special.

A possible way out is to look at those events (skills,
activities, titles) which we can ascribe to teachers, and
those characteristics (location, size, classification of
child, how time is spent) which can be ascribed to schools,
in the special domain. Except for location, it is not
possible to find a single event or characteristic that cannot

be found in non-special education i.e. in mainstream schooling. Furthermore, if we look at the ideology that may be said to underpin special education, is it more than a collection of principles drawn from other disciplines? Where can be found the tenets of its own philosophical base?

If there is not a separate philosophy of special education, and the case has yet to be established, then we have the first of what is a whole list of paradoxes in the field, namely, that special is separate because it is called special but it draws on the field of normal education to define its existence. This is illustrated more explicitly when those in special education refer to the special curriculum. Let us put aside for the time being what we mean by the term 'curriculum' and whether if we call something a 'special curriculum' then we are not talking about the curriculum as defined in education in general, but something different altogether.

It might be argued that the special curriculum is of two kinds: the provision of such aids as ramps for wheelchairs and the way material is presented for children to learn. If these exemplify the special curriculum then why in the provision of bicycle racks for children in ordinary schools do we not call these 'aids' special? If we think that special children learn differently from other children in ordinary schools, what evidence can we offer? The physically handicapped learn to read with the same set of common difficulties as most other children; braille for the blind is but another learning aid and like the computer is going to be for all children who require it; some children in special schools learn more slowly than others but all of us, no matter how bright we are, have a different learning pace for different things to be learned and understood. The watered-down ordinary curriculum provided for ESN(M) children in special schools is not a different, special curriculum, it is just watered-down (with possibly lowered expectations on the part of the teacher). The training programme provided for the severely mentally handicapped parallels exactly the early training we provide for all normal children from birth onwards (the only difference is the body size of the child).

If the problems associated with defining special education appear to be complex then the reader might try to define other terms in the present special vocabulary like 'disabled' or 'abnormal'. A common thread in all this is the way we find it necessary to polarize terms in some dualistic form. Good and bad or normal and abnormal are examples. There is no problem here if the two aspects are really two facets of something they share in common i.e. a human being may be defined in terms of both his physical and spiritual being (though the history of philosophy is one of discarded theories about the relationships between mind and body). But special education and mainstream education are not the essential elements in defining what we call education. Education is defined in two ways (1) the ideology of what is taught like a slice of the culture the children live in, or (2) the mechanics of the system, i.e. the way we group children into age-related classes and determined range of learning ability, for a particular age span in their lives (5-16 years), and located in places we call schools. Children in special schools are those who because of exceptional body growth, mental development, or social behaviour, are set outside this system of normal education (in fact help to define the boundaries of what we call normal), or to be more precise, are set outside by criteria set up by individual societies. Special education is defined, therefore, in terms of where it fails to match up to education as defined by that provided in ordinary schools. Hence from this process we find a dualistic pattern of 'educational' response to children but unlike the philosophers we do have a means of connecting one with another.

The first method is simply to educate all children in a common community (or school) but to do this the style of education in ordinary schools, defined by virtue of the exclusion of children we call special, has to change so that the organisation of education in mainstream is altered. Where the attitudes of teachers are in this direction then we are presently seeing some of the best educational innovation in education today. But we need to do something about the language that has grown up and which has become identified with children educationally segregated. First, we need to drop the word special as it is applied to children, teachers, departments, schools, administrators, advisers, tutors, qualifications, and not least, HMI. There is nothing to stop a special needs teacher being called a 'curriculum support teacher', and so forth, throughout the whole institution of special education. And here, we stumble on another paradox. The 1981 Education Act is supposed to maximise the opportunities of a certain group of children to be educated normally, but the provisions of the Act now legally secure the dualism as children are now labelled normal or statemented. A result of the Act is to increase the numbers of LEA personnel working in special education so that in the past two years we have seen a ten percent increase in special administrators, advisers and psychologists. As the bureaucracy increases so we observe the waiting lists for special schools grow longer and longer. What we do not as yet see is a new orientation in the kind of teacher we are training. What is needed is not the present kind of training plus some later specialisation (for example, in special education), nor a special element in initial training, but an initial training that encompasses a different style of attitudes towards learning, different techniques in classroom management and organisation, and an ability to make and respond to a wide range of educational needs as represented by children in 'ordinary' schools.

The Warnock Report recommended that initial teacher training should include a 'special education element' (the first dualistic statement) and that teachers should be taught child development with a recognition that children have different patterns and rates of individual development (the second dualistic statement). The theory of child development is based on the notion of skills of the average child at a given age. All developmental tests of children are geared to this. We teach individual differences, not as normal processes, but as derivatives from the average. Classes in schools are, certainly in primary education, geared round the normal average child. The question then becomes, how much deviation can we allow before establishing a cut-off point (which secures a place in a special school) when children can be described in a different language. This language changes over time but the linguistic labels serve a common purpose: to take out of ordinary education certain children. Hence the 'mentally subnormal' of history is the 'educationally subnormal' of recent times to the child with 'special educational needs' of today. The 'HP Form' of yesterday is replaced by the certificate of difference of today, the 'Statement'.

The effect on teachers of the concept of the 'normal average' is that they are trained to gear learning, expectations, rewards and punishments, to this norm. Hence, with learning to read, a child has only to be two years behind his chronological age on a norm-referenced reading test for him to be introduced to a system out of the normal: to people engaged in an exercise on learning failure, like remedial teachers and some psychologists; to a curriculum that other normal children do not follow, a special or remedial curriculum. They may find themselves attending establishments that are not part of normal schools, e.g. reading centres, and if the norm deviancy is measured in IQ terms then they are likely to be totally removed from ordinary education. This deficit model of managing norm deviancy could be replaced by a model of contextual learning for children but where will teachers learn this if the 'special educational element' is geared to a knowledge of practice and skills in education outside normal schools?

Until the term 'special' is dropped altogether from the educational vocabulary then training, services, skills, resources will continue to be seen in terms of development for *competence and ability* in ordinary education and *incompetence and inability* in special education with the overtones for unsuccessful learning that the latter has, and the effect this has on children and the parents of these children (Tomlinson 1983).

References

Advisory Committee on the Supply and Education of Teachers (1982) *The Initial Teacher Training System.* DES: London

Advisory Committee on the Supply and Education of Teachers. (1984a) *Teacher Training and Special Educational Needs*. DES, London

Advisory Committee on the Supply and Education of Teachers (1984b) *The In-Service Education and Training of School Teachers.* DES: London

Advisory Committee on the Supply and Training of Teachers. (1978) *Making Inset Work.* DES: London

Ainscow, M. and Muncey, J. (1983) Learning difficulties in the primary school: an in-service initiative. *Remedial Education.* 18, No. 3

Apter, S. J. (1982) *Troubled Children - Troubled Systems* . Pergamon: Oxford

Aspin, D. (1982) Towards a concept of human being as a basis for a philosophy of special education. *Education Review*. 34 No. 2

Audit Commission. (1984) Report obtainable from 1, Vincent Square, London S.W.1

Bandura, A. (1969) Social learning theory of identificatory processes. In: Goslin, D. A. (ed.) *Handbook of Socialisation Theory and Research.* Rand McNally: Chicago

Barker, R. G., Wright, B.A., Meyerson, D and Gornick, M. R. (1953) *Adjustment to Physical Handicap and Illness : A Survey of the Social Psychology of Physique and Disability* Social Science Research Council: New York

Barr, J. (1983) *Evaluation*. In: Booth, T. *Eradicating Handicap*. E241 Course, Unit 14. Open University Press. Milton Keynes

Blatt, B. (1972) The legal rights of the mentally retarded. *Syracuse Law Review.* 991 991-994

Booth, T. (1981) Demystifying integration. In: Swann, W. (ed.) *The Practice of Special Education*. Blackwells: Oxford

Booth, T. (1982) *Handicap is Social* . Open University Unit E241, No. 13 Special Needs in Education. Open University Press: Milton Keynes

Booth, T. and Potts, P. (1983) *Integrating Special Education* Basil Blackwell: Oxford

Booth, T. and Statham, J. (ed.), (1982) *The Nature of Special Education*. Croom Helm: London

Booth, T., Potts, P. and Swann, W. (1982) *An Alternative System: A Special Imagination.* Special Needs in Education, Unit 16. Open University Press: Milton Keynes

Booth, T., Potts, P. and Swann, W. (1983) *Special Needs In Education*. Unit 16., Open University Press: Milton Keynes

Brennan, W. K. (1982) *Changing Special Education*. Open University Press: Milton Keynes

Brennan, W. (1974) *Shaping the Education of Slow Learners*. Routledge and Kegan Paul: London

Chazan, M. (1964) The incidence and nature of maladjustment among children in schools for the educationally subnormal. *Brit. J. Educ. Psychol.*, 34 292-304

Clunies-Ross, L. and Wimhurst, S. (1983) *The Right Balance: provision for slow learners in secondary schools*. NFER - Nelson: Windsor.

Committee on Child Health Services. (1976)*Fit for the Future* (Court Report). Cmnd. 6684. HMSO: London

Cope, C. and Anderson, E. (1977) *Special Units in Ordinary Schools*, Studies in Education No.6, Institute of Education: London University

Coventry LEA (1982) *Pupils with Special Educational Needs : Handbook*. Coventry

Dahmen, K., Breitenbach, D., Mitter, W. and Wilhelmi, H. (eds.) (1984) *Comprehensive Schools in Europe*, Bohlam Vetlag Koln: Wien

Davis, F. (1964) Deviance disavowal: the management of strained interaction by the physically handicapped. In: Becker, H.S. (ed.) *The Other Side*, Free Press: New York

Department of Education and Science (1975) *Discovery of Children Requiring Special Education and the Assessment of their Needs*. HMSO: London

Department of Education and Science. (1978) *Special Needs in Education*, (Warnock Report) HMSO: London

Department of Education and Science. (1983) *The School Curriculum*, H.M.S.O. London

Department of Education and Science. (1983) *Young Children With Special Educational Needs* : An HMI survey of education arrangements in 61 nurseries. HMSO London

Department of Education and Science (1983) *Teaching Qualities* HMSO. London.

Department of Education and Science. (1984) *Initial Teacher Training:Approval of Courses*. HMSO : London A Note

Dodgson, E. (1984) *Motherland : West Indian Women in Britain in the 1950's*, Heinemann : London

Family Focus (1982) 'Assessing Special Needs - parents should be involved'. *Where*, No. 183

Fish, J. (1984) 'The Future of the Special School' In: Bowers, T. (ed.) *Management and the Special School*. Croom Helm: London

Fox, M. (1975) *They Get This Training, but they don't really know how to feel*.

Fuller, P., Poon, P., and Southgate, T. (1983) Microcomputers at Ormerod School. *Special Education : Forward Trends*, Vol.10, No.3, September

Fuller, P. and Southgate, T. (1984) The introduction and management of microcomputors in special schools. Conference Paper : *The Computer as an Aid for Those with Special Needs*. Sheffield Polytechnic.

Galloway, D. and Goodwin, C. (1979) *Educating Slow-learning And Maladjusted Children*, Longman: London

Garnett, E.J. (1976) Special children in a comprehensive. *Special Education : Forward Trends,* No. 3, Vol. pp. 8-11

Goldenberg, E., Russell, S., and Carter, C. (1984)*Computers, Education and Special Needs*, Addison-Wesley: Mass.

Greater London Association for the Disabled. (1984) *After 16: the education of young people with special needs*, GLAD: London

Green, F., Hart, R., McCall, C. and Staples I. (1983) *Microcomputers in Special Education*. Schools Council Programme 4. Longman: York

Hammond, R. (1983) *Computers and Your Child*, Century Pub: London

Hansard (1981) Education Bill. Special Standing Committee 18.02.81, Cols. 5 and 6

Hansard (1982) House of Commons written answers. 20.07.82. Cols. 130-131

Hargreaves, D.H. (1984) *Improving Secondary Schools*.Report of the Committee on the Curriculum and Organization of Secondary Schools. Inner London Education Authority

Hegarty, S. and Pocklington, K. (1981) *Educating Pupils With Special Needs in the Ordinary School*. NFER/NELSON: Windsor

Hegarty, S. and Pocklington, P. (1982) *Integration in Action* NFER/Nelson: Windsor

Heron, T.E. and Harris, K.C. (1982) *The Educational Consultant*. Allyn and Bacon

Hewitt, S. (1970) *The Family and the Handicapped Child*. A study of cerebral palsied children in their homes. Allen and Unwin: London

Hodgson, A., Clunies-Ross, L. and Hegarty, S. (1984)*Learning Together* : teaching pupils with special needs in the ordinary school. NFER/Nelson: Windsor

Jaffe, J. (1967) "What's in a name" - attitudes towards disabled persons. *Personnel and Guidance Journal*. No. 45 557-60

Jones, Neville J. (1983) Policy change and innovation for special needs in Oxfordshire. *Oxford Review of Education* 9 No. 3

Jones, Neville J. (1985) School welfare and pupils with special educational needs. In: Ribbens, P. (ed.), *Welfare and Schools*. In press

Jones, Neville J. and Jones, E.M. (1981) Oxfordshire looks towards the future. *Special Education*. *Forward Trends*. 8 No. 2. June

Jones, R.L. (1966) Research on the special education teacher and special education teaching. *Exceptional Children*. 33, No. 4, 251-6

Jones, R.L., Gottfried, N.W. and Owens, A. (1966) The social distance of the exceptional: a study at the high school level. *Exceptional Children*. 32 551-6

Lawton, D. (1980) *The Politics of the School Curriculum*. Routledge and Kegan Paul: London

Lawton, D. (1983) *Curriculum Studies and Educational Planning* Hodder and Stoughton: London

Lewis, I. and Vulliamy, G. (1981) The social context of educational practices In: Barton, L. and Tomlinson, S. *Special Education : Policy, Practice and Social Issues*. Harper and Row: London

Loxley, D. (1978) 'Community Psychology'. In: Gillham, B. (ed.) *Reconstructing Educational Psychology*.Croom Helm: London

McCullough, M. (1972) *1-2-3 and Away : Teachers Manual*. Hart-Davis: St Albans

Measor, L. and Woods, P. (1984) Cultivating the middle ground: teachers and school ethos. *Research in Education* No. 31

Meyerson, D. (1956) Somatopsychology of physical disability In: Cruickshank, W.M. (ed.), *Psychology of Exceptional Children and Youth.* Prentice Hall: New Jersey

Ministry of Education. (1955) *Report of the Committee on Maladjusted Children.* (Underwood Report). HMSO: London

Mittler, P. (1979) Research into special education.*Trends in Education.* 3, 17-22

Mittler, P. (1981) 'Training for the 21st. Century'. *Special Education : Forward Trends*. 8.2

Muncey, J. and Ainscow, M. (1982) 'Launching SNAP in Coventry' *Special Education : Forward Trends*. 10 3

Mussen, P.H. and Barker, R.G. (1944) Attitudes towards cripples. *Journal of Abnormal and Social Psychology*. 39, 251-255

National Association of Remedial Education. (1979) NARE: Stafford

National Association of Remedial Education. (1984) 'Special Needs: Admin Changes are Not Enough'. *Education*. 20 January

National Fund for Research into Crippling Disease. (1976) *Integration of the Disabled*. Report of the Snowdon Working Party

Oder, P. (1984) Hard and soft technology for education and communication for disabled people. Conference paper: Australia

O'Shea, T. and Self, J. (1983) *Learning and Teaching With Computers - Artificial Intelligence in Education*. Harvester Press: Brighton

Papert, S. (1980) *Mindstorms.* Harvester Press: Brighton

Peter, M. (1984) 'A Hard Act to Follow'. *TES*, 30 March

Poon, P. (1981) Strategies for improving the communication rate of people with severe physical impairments. *RADAR:* London

Pringle M.K. (1974) *The Needs of Children*. Hutchinson: London

Pritchard, D.G.(1963) *Education and the Handicapped 1760-1960* Routledge and Kegan Paul: London

Quicke, J.C. (1978) Rogerian psychology and 'non-directive' counselling in schools. *Educational Research*. 20 No.3, 192-200

Report of the Committee on Local Authority & Allied Personal Services. (Seebohm Report) Cmnd, 3703, HMSO : London.

Report of the Committee of Enquiry into the Education of Handicapped Children and Young People. (1978) *Special Educational Needs.* Cmnd 7212. (Warnock Report) HMSO: London

Reynolds, D. and Sullivan, M. (1981) 'The effects of school: a radical faith re-stated' . In: Gillham, B. (ed.) *Problem Behaviour in the Secondary School.* Croom Helm: London

Rogers, R. (1984 *Crowther to Warnock.* Heinemann: London.

Rutter, M., Maughan, B., Mortimore, P. and Ouston, J. (1979) *Fifteen Thousand Hours.* Open Books: London

Rutter, M., Tizard, J. and Whitmore, K. (1970) *Education, Health and Behaviour.* Longman: London

Sabatino. D. (1972) Resource rooms: the renaissance in special education. *Journal of Special Education.* 6 No.4, 335-47

Sayer, J. (ed.), (1982) *Staffing our Secondary Schools : A Quest for Criteria.* Secondary Heads Association: London

Sayer, J. (1983) A Comprehensive school for all In: Booth, T. and Potts, P. (eds.), *Integrating Special Education.* Blackwell: Oxford

Sayer, J. *Training for Diversity.* Adapted with permission from Times Educational Supplement article. 14 September 1984.

Scottish Education Department.(1978) *The Education of Pupils with Learning Difficulties.* H.M.I. Scotland

Scottish Microelectronics Development Programme. (1984) *Microspecial Pack.* Glasgow

Smith, C. (1983) *Special Education Aspects of P.G.C.E. Courses.* Unpublished research project. Birmingham University

Stanovich, K.E., Cunningham, A.E. and Feeman, D. (1984) Intelligence, cognitive skills, and early reading progress. *Reading Research Quarterly,* XIX No. 3, Spring

Sutherland, G. and Sharp, S. (1980) 'The fursst official psychologist in the wurrld'; aspects of the professionalisation of psychology in twentieth century Britain.' *History of Science,* 18

Sutherland, G. (1984) *Ability, Merit and Measurement.* Clarendon Press: Oxford

Swann, W. (ed.), (1982) *The Practice of Special Education.* Blackwell: Oxford

Swann, W. (1983) 'Curriculum Principles for Integration' In: Booth, T. and Potts. P. (eds.) *Integrating Special Education.* Blackwell: Oxford

Swann, W., Bookbinder, G. and O'Hagan, F. (1984)*The New Laws on Special Education.* Open University E241, Special Needs in Education, Supplement. Open University Publications: Milton Keynes

Swann, W. (1985) 'Integration of Special Needs: analysis of recent statistics of pupils in special schools.' *Oxford Review of Education, 11.1.*

Tattum, D. (1982) *Disruptive Pupils in Schools and Units.* Wiley: Chichester

TES, (1983) 11 March

Thomas, D. (1978)   *The Social Psychology of Childhood Disability.*   Methuen: London
Thomas, D. (1982) *The Experience of Handicap.*   Methuen: London
Tomlinson, S. (1981).   *Educational Subnormality : A Study in Decision-Making.*   Routledge & Kegan Paul: London
Tomlinson, S. (1982).   *A Sociology of Special Education.*   Routledge & Kegan Paul : London
Tomlinson, S. (1983) Why Assess - and Who Benefits? *Journal of Special Education.*   10 No. 4
Westwood, L.J. (1967) The role of the teacher. *Educational Research.*   9 122-133
Warnock, M. (1979) Children with special needs: the Warnock Report. *Brit. Med. Journal.*   1 667-668
Warnock, M. (1983a) 'Personal'. *TES,* 11 November.
Weber, K. (1982) *The Teacher is the Key* : A practical guide for teaching adolescents with learning difficulties. Open University Press: Milton Keynes
Widlake, P, (1984) *How to Reach the Hard to Teach.*   Open University Press: Milton Keynes
Wilding, P. (1982) *Professional Power and Social Welfare.*   Routledge and Kegan Paul: London
Wood Report (1929) *Report of the Joint Departmental Committee on Mental Deficiency.*   Board of Education and Board of Control, HMSO: London
Yuker, H.E., Block, J.R. and Campbell, W.J. (1960) *A Scale to Measure Attitudes towards Disabled Persons.*   Human Resources Foundation: New York

Special Needs Diploma Structure: Two-Credit Course

Part One   E241 Special Needs in Education (half credit)

Part Two   A compatible Open University Education course
              (half credit)

Part Three   E806 A project based full credit course built
              around three new text books

              Curricula for all (Prevention of learning
              difficulties pack)

              Disaffection and the school curriculum

              Disability and the school curriculum

              Projects will be studied at following levels:

                  Classroom interaction

                  School policy and curriculum development

                  LEA and national policy

Preventing Learning Difficulties

Section 1 Reconnecting Remedial Education

Session 1   Introduction: When and Why is Learning
              Difficult?

Session 2   Choosing an Approach Towards Learning
              Difficulties

Section 5 Organising the schools

Session 16   Financing schools and assessing priorities

Session 17   Groupings

Session 18   Planning time and timetables

Session 19   Controlling the curriculum

Section 6 Conclusion and Review

Session 20   Conclusion and Review

APPENDIX TWO

INVITED SEMINAR, OXFORD UNIVERSITY

21-23 JUNE 1984

                              PARTICIPANTS AND WRITERS

Gill Ager   Warden, Teachers Centre
                              Hounslow

Marion Blythman   Senior Lecturer
                              Moray House, Edinburgh

Tony Booth   Lecturer in Education
                              Open University

Katrin Fitzherbert   Social Science Research Council
                              West London College of FE

Michael Jones   Principal, Wantage School
                              Oxfordshire

Elizabeth Jones   HMI
                              Department of Education and Science

Neville Jones   Principal Educational Psychologist
                              Oxfordshire

Denis Mongon	Advisory Teacher Inner London Education Authority
Dominique Paty	Direction des Colleges Ministry of Education, Paris
Margaret Peter	Editor Special Education
Patricia Potts	Lecturer in Education Open University
John Quicke	Lecturer in Education Sheffield University
Norman Rea	Lecturer in Education University of York
John Sayer	Principal, Banbury School Oxfordshire
Colin Smith	Lecturer in Education Birmingham University
Tim Southgate	Headmaster, Ormerod School Oxfordshire
Will Swann	Lecturer in Education Open University
David Thomas	Senior Lecturer in Special Education University of Liverpool
Kate Torkington	Community Education Development Centre, Coventry
Prof. Klaus Wedell	Institute of Education University of London
Chloe West	AEO Special Education Oxfordshire
Nanette Whitbread	President NATFHE Leicester Polytechnic